The Author Can Be Contacted For
Interviews
Or Questions at:

1-800-400-0577

LONG-TERM CARE PLANNING

Assuring Choice, Independence, & Financial Security

ALLEN HAMM

includes Interviews with Financial Experts

LONG-TERM CARE PLANNING

Assuring Choice, Independence, & Financial Security

ALLEN HAMM

includes **Interviews with Financial Experts**

The purpose of this publication is to provide accurate information on the subject of long-term care planning and insurance. The publisher and author are not engaged in rendering legal or accounting service and/or advice. The author's experience is in one narrow aspect of financial planning: long-term care planning and insurance. Because the industry is in constant change, and information and benefits may vary from state to state, the author recommends seeking professional advice from a local, competent financial professional trained in long-term care planning prior to acting on any advice whatsoever given in this book.

The author has made every attempt to give credit where credit is due with regard to material in this book. Much of the material is based on the author's personal experience and opinion. The author and the publisher will not accept liability or responsibility to any person or entity with respect to any loss and/or damage caused directly or indirectly by the information presented in this book.

Any attempt to litigate against the author or publisher with malice will be met with a position of defense and offense that uses the fullest extent of the law to recuperate any damages to the reputation of the author or the publisher, including, but not limited to monetary, time, and emotional resources.

CFPs, CPAs, and Estate Planning Attorneys may earn Continuing Education Accreditation. For more information: 1-800-400-0577.

ISBN: 0-9764189-2-4

Published by:	Plan Ahead, Inc.
Cover and Interior Design:	Quin Coursey, QuinCoursey@comcast.net
Interior Photos:	©PhotoDisc/Getty Images ©Dynamic Graphics, ©Banana Stock

Dedication

*Dedicated to my father, who continues to inspire me by example.
And to my sons, Brian and Alex, to whom I strive to do the same.*

Acknowledgments

This book exists because of the encouragement of my wife, Eileen. During the entire project, she reinforced the importance of subduing my "humbleness" and concentrating on getting this information into the hands of American families. Her personal perspectives are given in *Chapter 5: Why Is Long-Term Care a Woman's Issue?*

Thanks to my mentor, Bob Bingham, CFP®, who inspired me by example to formally develop an approach to solving an important area of financial and estate planning. His influence resulted in the development of the **Comprehensive Planning Approach** to long-term care.

My appreciation to attorney Harley Gordon, President of the Corporation for Long-Term Care Certification, Inc. (www.ltc-cltc.com) for allowing us to use material from his many years of experience in LTC Planning.

Thanks to Jesse Slome, editor of Long-Term Care Insurance Sales Strategies (www.ltcsales.com) for allowing us to use the interview in *Chapter 14,* statistical materials, and quotes from his publications.

The technical aspects of Medicaid explained in *Chapter 4* were put into laymen's terms by Julie Fiedler, Estate Planning Attorney. The financial and estate planning processes outlined in Part 2 were written with the assistance of Steve Bell, CFP®. He also wrote *Chapter 18: Long-Term Care Planning and Insurance Myths.*

Thanks to all the financial professionals who agreed to be interviewed for *Chapter 19.* We regret that this edition includes only a fraction of the interviews generously given.

Thanks to Quin Coursey, our graphic designer. She is not only the most professional person in her field, but also the most patient person in the world. She worked with my perfectionism for 2 years and never once raised her voice!

TABLE OF CONTENTS

PREFACE
Long-Term Care is America's True Health Care Crisis

In the next decade, the healthy lifestyles and medical advances that will enable millions of Americans to live well beyond 100 years may also pose the greatest threat to the financial security and retirement plans of the most prosperous generation in history. Our newest and biggest challenge in health care will be to physically and psychologically care for those who have managed to live well beyond today's life expectancy.

It's been estimated that the number of people requiring long-term care will double in the next three decades. This means that more than 28 million people could need help with the basic activities of daily living—tasks such as getting dressed, which are now performed with ease, will require assistance from others. Unable to live independently, these large numbers of people in need of care will create tremendous demand for new health care solutions in the first half of the 21st century. This new health care challenge—long-term care—will dwarf our current problems of financing physician and hospital care.

Who will provide this care? Where will the care take place? Who will pay the bills? The long-term care industry is working to find the answers to many of these questions. Soon, planning ahead for long-term care will become as common as creating a will.

One option for paying for the costs of care is long-term care insurance. We devote several chapters of this book to a discussion of this option. If you haven't already purchased long-term care insurance, we encourage you to wait the few hours it will take to read this book. Then, speak with your financial professional *first*—your financial planner, estate planning attorney, or CPA—not an insurance agent. Your financial professional can assist you in planning ahead for long-term care by considering your options within the context of your personal and financial objectives. This process of integrating your plan for long-term care with your personal and financial objectives is called the ***Comprehensive Planning Approach*** to long-term care.

Attempting to plan ahead for long-term care without heeding this advice, could be a major mistake. Why? Because the LTC Planning industry is heavily influenced by the insurance industry. Traditional insurance agents often use a *single sales approach,* and attempt to convince you that long-term care insurance is the only option for paying for long-term care. The critical difference between the *Comprehensive Planning Approach* and the *single sales approach* can mean the difference between success and failure for your financial and estate plan, and for your legacy.

After you read the information presented in these pages, you will have the knowledge you need to ask meaningful questions and make an informed decision about how to create an effective plan for long-term care.

INTRODUCTION

In my 18 years of LTC Planning experience, I have heard hundreds of painful stories about the effects of long-term care. The following story recounts my personal experiences. My purpose in sharing these observations with you is to communicate the basis and foundation for my strong belief in planning ahead for long-term care.

For those who are anxious to learn the specifics of planning ahead, I invite you to move ahead to **Part 1: Understanding Long-Term Care.**

LONG-TERM CARE IS A FAMILY AFFAIR

*I pondered my family's lack of knowledge
about long-term care planning. How could
we know so much about most financial issues,
but know so little about such a critical part
of the financial and estate planning process?*

— Allen Hamm

My family has confronted long-term care twice in 2 separate generations. These experiences influenced me to choose a career in long-term care planning and to write this book. These experiences are not uncommon: millions of other American families will face similar scenarios in the coming decades.

I was raised in a traditional American family. As I grew up, I dreamed of going into business for myself, or maybe even buying the small company my grandfather owned. He had built a successful business that supported many of his family members for several decades.

By the late 1970s, when my grandfather was 72, we began to notice a slight change in his mental alertness. Since he appeared to be managing the company without any problems, we paid little attention to it at first. But we began to take it seriously when we received complaints from his suppliers about late invoice payments. Then one day, we got a call from a close family friend and the owner of one of the businesses that supplied his materials. "Allen," he said, "your grandfather's check just bounced." There was shock in his voice, and a dead silence on my end of the phone. My grandfather had always been meticulous about keeping his accounts organized.

Over the next few months, my family was subjected to a painful series of discoveries about the state of my grandfather's mental health and his company's finances. We learned that he was suffering from the early onset of Alzheimer's Disease. The condition was causing him to slowly lose control of both his personal life and his business affairs. By the time we discovered the true dimensions of his problems, it was too late. His once thriving company was in financial trouble.

Within two years of his diagnosis, my grandfather required a level of long-term care our family could no longer provide at home. We contacted Medicare, expecting that as a hard-working American businessman who had made a positive contribution to society and the economy, he would be well covered for whatever medical and custodial care services he might require. What we learned was almost as upsetting as our original discoveries: neither his Medicare nor his Medicare Supplement policy offered coverage for long-term custodial care. And although he had lost most of his assets in the demise of his business, he still had too much money to qualify for Medicaid, the welfare program.

Prior to my grandfather's health problems, my parents had been diligently saving for an early retirement. But after my grandfather's mental and financial decline, they were forced to cash in their retirement savings to fund quality care for my grandfather. He spent the last four years of his life in a private pay nursing home.

After the loss of my grandfather's business, I pondered my family's lack of knowledge about long-term care planning. How could we know so much about most financial issues, but know so little about such a critical part of the financial and estate planning process? I became intensely interested in the subject of long-term care and how our country funds this growing problem.

In the mid-1980's, I moved to California—something that I had been considering for several years. Moving 2,000 miles away from my family was one of the most difficult decisions I've ever made. Dad had always been my mentor. Strong, wise, and patient, he had always been able to say or do just the right thing at the right moment. He had never been wealthy, but he taught us family values and the importance of planning for our financial future. As an adult, I admired his positive attitude and tenacity, especially after experiencing adversity and set-backs. Slowly, with hard work and integrity, he built a separate company of his own. Inspired by his example, and the tragedy that long-term care brought to my grandfather's last years, I fulfilled my own dream of starting a business—a company that specializes in assisting people with planning ahead for long-term care *before* the need arises.

After becoming a specialist in long-term care planning, I worked with my parents' financial advisor to evaluate LTC Planning options that would be suitable for their situation. After experiencing my grandfather's long-term care situation, I didn't expect my parents to react enthusiastically to a conversation about their own potential need for long-term care. Few parents want to talk with their children about the possibility of becoming dependent on someone else or requiring assistance with their physical care. However, we all agreed that it made sense to put plans in place that would give them choices we didn't have with my grandfather—plans that would protect the assets they had worked so hard to rebuild after his need for care. They chose LTC insurance as their option, and I returned to California pleasantly surprised that they had agreed to plan ahead with no resistance.

About three years after his LTC insurance policy went into effect, my father was diagnosed with mild Parkinson's Disease. Had he been diagnosed years earlier or waited longer to purchase LTC insurance, he would not have been able to obtain coverage. As we'll explain later in this book, the ability to obtain LTC insurance is based on a person's health at the time they apply for coverage, and a person with Parkinson's Disease will not qualify for coverage.

My father was in his mid-60s when his symptoms started with a slight tremor in his left arm. The prognosis was progressive neurological deterioration and, over a period of years, severe physical and cognitive disabilities could be expected. But in the short term, he remained active with his family, business, and church, and our hopes were high that a cure for Parkinson's Disease would be found within his lifetime.

Busy with my own family and running our company, I tried to keep an objective eye on Dad's condition with frequent phone calls from 2,000 miles away. Fortunately, my brother lives in the same area as my parents, and is also able to keep me updated on Dad's physical and mental health.

During my semi-annual visits, I noticed that physically, his tremor seemed to be slowly getting worse. I respected him too much to pry into his psychological health, but my frequent calls allowed me to monitor his mood for signs of depression or fatigue. By this time, my experience in handling several LTC insurance claims made me well aware of the signs of many types of health conditions, particularly mental and neurological disorders.

Shortly before Dad turned 70, my wife, two sons and I attended an eagerly anticipated family reunion. Seeing him for the first time in almost a year, Dad seemed unusually tired and melancholy. Even his grandsons failed to spark his usual enthusiasm. Concerned about him, I suggested that the two of us have a private talk in the backyard. We sat down at an old picnic table where we'd had many family cookouts and private talks. I asked him to open up to me.

His eyes began to water, something I'd never seen. He's a warm person, but has always been very much in control of his emotions. He looked away and began to talk.

"Your mom doesn't know, and I don't know how to tell her. Or even you…but here goes…I'm in debt. We're on the verge of losing everything. We're behind on our house payment and the rental property mortgages. The banks are no longer willing to finance our projects. When I was diagnosed with Parkinson's, I knew that I only had a short period of time to get your mother set-up, to make sure she wouldn't have to worry once the Parkinson's took control. I rushed with some major business decisions; I made some missteps; I took on too many projects. I've lost control of where we are financially."

At first, I couldn't accept what he was telling me. I tried to reassure him, the way he had always reassured me. We were in the family backyard, at our familiar picnic table, but I felt as disconnected as if I were watching a movie or having a bad dream. I felt a certain level of panic, followed by—I'm ashamed to say—a sense of betrayal. Could this be my mentor, the man I had always looked up to, allowing something to get so out of control? And how could we repeat something so shockingly familiar to what we had been through years earlier with my grandfather?

It was a heartbreaking moment, magnified by the realization and the fear of what could happen to any of us, including me. In the midst of all those overwhelming emotions, there was not as much comfort as I had expected in knowing that he had a written plan for long-term care, with an LTC insurance policy in force. As much as the coverage will spare us from the financial consequences of a future long-term care need, I realized for a second time that the worst part of this issue called "aging" is the emotional side—watching how it humbles the people we love, and how it often affects their ability to be as emotionally and rationally strong as they had been in the past.

Several years have passed since that afternoon when I learned once again how fast life can change. Fortunately, these past few years have been good to our family: my dad's Parkinson's has progressed more slowly. And after developing a plan of action as a family, the worst of his financial problems have also been resolved. They still have their rental property, although the family home had to be sold. He has yet to collect a dime on his LTC insurance policy, as he is very fond of reminding me. The last time we visited him, he seemed like his old self again. Naturally, I still worry about the way Parkinson's will affect his future. But we feel very blessed that he is still able to live an independent and productive life.

My family's experiences are ones that many families are experiencing this very minute. And these types of experiences will continue to affect families in the coming decades, as we learn to respond to this ever-increasing problem of the new health care crisis called long-term care.

PART 1 *Understanding Long-Term Care*

Education gives you the clarity to believe only half of what you hear. Experience gives you the power to know which half.

— Jerome Perryman
(paraphrased)

PART 1:
Understanding Long-Term Care

Some of the reluctance to face planning ahead for long-term care is due to the general confusion and misinformation surrounding the issue. It's easier to address other aspects of financial and estate planning because the issues are black and white—for instance, we know we need to plan for what our death will mean to our family. But planning for chronic illness and frailty? These issues are almost always accompanied by strong emotions of denial, anger, and fear.

Thinking ahead to a time when we might no longer function independently **is** depressing. But planning for long-term care is imperative. Without a written plan, our families will be forced to make painful and sometimes urgent decisions—decisions about the type of care needed, who will provide the services, where the services will be provided, and who will pay for the care.

Planning ahead means not waiting until a long-term care need arises, and then attempting to plan for someone's care. Planning now will allow us to focus on *emotionally* supporting our loved ones if they ever need care in the future.

The five chapters in Part 1 address these key issues and provide you with a foundation for understanding long-term care.

Chapter 1

What is Long-Term Care?

*Long-term custodial care for the chronically ill
may prove to be the most challenging and expensive of
the several demographic time bombs America faces.*

— Stephen Moses
President, Center for Long-Term Care Reform, Inc.

Long-term care, in the broadest sense, is defined as a need for assistance with the normal activities of daily living. Long-term care can be due to a disability or impairment, whether it be physical or mental in nature. We define *true* long-term care as care needed for a period *greater than 100 days.* We define short-term care as care needed for a period of *less than 100 days.*

Various definitions of long-term care can be found throughout the industry. For example, traditional insurance agents will attempt to scare you into believing that care needed for less than 100 days is a serious financial risk. This can result in a focus on "small dollars," while placing too little emphasis on the risk of "large dollars" caused by the need for *true* long-term care. Short-term care is financially and emotionally inconvenient; long-term care is financially and emotionally devastating. The problem to solve is **long-term care.**

ACTIVITIES OF DAILY LIVING

The first part of our long-term care definition states that a person needs "assistance." Whether or not a person needs assistance is determined in a variety of ways. Usually, a person's ability to perform basic "activities of daily living" is assessed to determine the need for care. Activities of daily living, commonly called *ADLs,* include functions most of us perform each day, including such activities as: eating, bathing, dressing, and toileting. Performing ADLs can be broadly defined as "the normal management of daily life without causing harm to oneself or others." Chronic difficulty with performing two or

FAST FACTS:

- Individuals born during the baby boom generation began turning 60 in 2006.

- In the next few years, older people will outnumber younger people for the first time in history.

- Care for adults is on the verge of replacing child care as the number one dependent care issue.

- The over-85 age group is expected to triple as a percentage of the population by 2050.

- Many people will need care for the last two decades or more of their life.

- Short-term care is financially and emotionally inconvenient; long-term care is financially and emotionally devastating.

more ADLs independently is the normal definition of "needing assistance."

Incidental Activities of Daily Living

Another relevant term is "incidental activities of daily living," also known as *IADLs*. Examples of IADLs include such activities as cooking, cleaning, and running errands. While ADLs is a medical term used to describe and determine the need for assistance, IADLs is the term used to describe and determine the *convenience* services required as a result of ADL loss or impairment.

MENTAL IMPAIRMENT

The need for assistance may also be due to mental impairment. Memory loss, including conditions such as Alzheimer's Disease, is the most common reason people need long-term care services after age 70.

THE NEED FOR LONG-TERM CARE IS GROWING

The number of people needing long-term care is growing fast, and will continue to escalate over the next three decades. Three major trends that gain momentum as each year passes will have a phenomenal impact on health care in general, and long-term care in particular:

1. **You will likely live a long life.** "The Aging of America" is driven by the largest generation in history, the baby boomers. The sheer numbers—76 million Americans born between 1946 and 1964—have had a significant impact on modern society on every social and economic level. Individuals in this generation began to turn 60 in 2006. The implications are profound

because the odds of needing true long-term care begin to significantly increase in the years beyond age 60.

2. **Living a long life will probably result in the need for long-term care prior to dying.** Our current population is not only large in numbers, but also has a large percentage of "health conscious" people. A good diet and exercise has a positive effect on longevity. But our bodies and minds will still eventually wear out, only at a much slower pace.

   Breakthroughs in medical science may contribute to making a life to age 100 a common occurrence. Some experts predict that life expectancy could be pushed to 120 years, and possibly beyond. Ironically, many health conscious people will need care for the last two decades or more of their lives.

3. **It is unlikely your family will be able to provide your care.** Care for adults is on the verge of replacing child care as the number one dependent care issue. Older people will soon outnumber younger people for the first time in history.

   In the past, when a family member needed long-term care, other family members stepped in to fill the role of caregiver. It was usually women, including wives and daughters, who became the primary caregivers for immediate and extended family members.

   But the changing family structure is having a profound effect on our ability to assist one another. With more women entering the workforce and careers geographically separating most families, **paid** caregivers will soon provide the bulk of long-term care services.

Cost and Availability of Quality Services

The increase in the numbers of people needing care will have a profound effect on the cost and availability of services. And the availability of *quality* services is likely to be in proportion to our ability to pay for care. For this reason, long-term care services paid for with private dollars, either with personal assets or with long-term care (LTC) insurance, will access better quality of care in future years.

WHEN DO PEOPLE NEED LONG-TERM CARE?

Although we normally think of long-term care as a concern reserved only for the elderly, the need for long-term care can arise at any age and at any time. Most of us are aware of younger people who have needed care, usually due to an accident or a disabling illness.

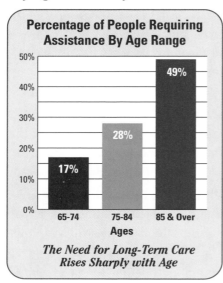

Percentage of People Requiring Assistance By Age Range

The Need for Long-Term Care Rises Sharply with Age

Middle-aged people can also suddenly lose the ability to care for themselves. In midlife, a need for long-term care normally results from conditions such as heart disease and strokes. Mental health conditions also become more prevalent during middle age.

But the reality is, the odds of needing long-term care and the duration of the need for long-term care services begin to increase drastically as we age. The vast majority of people needing care for five years or longer fall in the 60-and-older age group.

The most dramatic leap in the need for long-term care comes in the over-85 age group. Almost half of all people over age 85 require some form of care, either at home or in a facility. Long-term care is a serious societal issue because this age group is the fastest growing segment of the American population. The over-85 age group will triple as a percentage of the population by 2050.

WHAT ARE THE ODDS OF NEEDING LONG-TERM CARE?

Most available statistics regarding the odds of needing long-term care are wrong because they often include care needed for short periods of time.

One reliable, yet incomplete statistic comes from a recent study by the U.S. Department of Health and Human Services. The study reveals that of all people turning 65 this year, one in four will spend one year or longer in a nursing home. One in eleven will spend five years or longer in a nursing home.

But this statistic does not account for people who need care at home or care in an assisted living facility. When the environments of home care and assisted living care are factored in, it's estimated that there is a one in five chance of needing *true* long-term care during the average person's lifetime.

What about your individual odds of needing care? By analyzing your family's health history, you may be able to determine your chances of needing care. For example:

- Alzheimer's Disease or other forms of dementia in your family: Long-term care due to memory loss is not only the number one cause of needing long-term care, but also the most costly.
- Neurological conditions in your family: Parkinson's Disease and other neurological disorders are a common reason for needing long-term care.
- Longevity in your family: A long life expectancy may indicate higher odds of needing care.

REDUCING YOUR ODDS

Taking a proactive approach toward life is the key to reducing your odds of needing long-term care.

Proven techniques for living a long, healthy life and reducing your odds of needing care include:

- **Staying active physically.** Even a minimum level of daily physical activity makes a significant difference.
- **Socializing.** Spend as much time as possible with family and friends. Become involved in activities that include others.
- **Eating with others.** Research has shown that having meals with other people offers multiple benefits. For example, people who eat together are more likely to eat more nutritious meals, which can help avoid both mental and physical problems. Eating together also offers the opportunity to socialize.
- **Continuously learning.** Challenge your mind daily. Working crossword puzzles, reading, and stretching your imagination, will contribute to a healthier state of mind, potentially reducing the odds of needing care due to mental problems, including loss of memory.

KEY POINTS

What is Long-Term Care?

➤ A person who needs long-term care requires assistance for an extended period of time—100 days or longer—with little chance for recovery.

➤ A person who needs short-term care requires assistance for a limited period of time—less than 100 days—with an expected outcome of full recovery.

➤ The need for long-term care is growing due to the aging of America, advances in medical science, and changes in the family structure.

➤ The need for long-term care can arise at younger ages due to an accident or disabling illness.

➤ The fastest growing segment of our population is the over age 85 group. Almost half of all people in this age group require some form of long-term care.

➤ Reduce your odds of needing care by taking a proactive approach toward life. Stay active physically and mentally. Socialize and have meals with other people.

Chapter 2 Where is Long-Term Care Received?

It's nice to be here. At my age it's nice to be anywhere.
— George Burns

A person in need of long-term care can be cared for in a variety of settings, including their home, an assisted living community, or a nursing home. The severity of the condition and the level of care required will dictate the environment in which a person's care can be safely and adequately received.

The ultimate goal of any type of care is to help the person maintain comfort, and, if possible, regain some or all of their ability to live independently.

LEVELS OF CARE

There are two broad levels of long-term care: *skilled* and *non-skilled*.

Skilled Care

Someone with an *acute condition* that requires intensive medical attention will normally require a short period of skilled care.

The care being described here would likely fall into the category of *short-term care* because the duration of the need for care is almost always less than 100 days.

The two objectives of skilled care are:

- Help the person with comfort and assistance, if the condition is terminal. This type of care is often referred to as *hospice care*.

or

- Assist the person during a recovery period.

Skilled care is sometimes covered by public and private health insurance programs and by Medicare. For example, the owner of a window cleaning company fell off a roof one morning and broke just about every bone in his body. The prognosis given by his physician: full recovery. He did fully recuperate, and his health insurance paid his medical expenses until he was back on his feet. He even went

FAST FACTS:

■ **57%** of all people with a disability rely exclusively on unpaid care from family or other informal caregivers at home.

■ Home care is projected to increase by **178%** by 2030.

■ Elderly patients who spend longer than two years in a nursing home rarely return home.

■ There was a **61%** increase in the number of assisted living communities built between 1998 and 2006.

■ Alzheimer's Disease afflicts about four million Americans; by 2025, this figure is projected to grow by **75%**.

into a nursing home for two weeks and the nursing home bill was covered by his health insurance. The level of care he needed was "skilled care" because his prognosis was full recovery, with the need for a short period of rehabilitation.

Non-Skilled Care

Most people in need of care receive non-skilled care, frequently called *custodial care*. This level of care is administered to a person who has a *chronic condition*, meaning they will not recover. Custodial care is most commonly received at home or in assisted living communities. Conditions such as Parkinson's Disease, Alzheimer's Disease, or simply the aging process can cause the need for custodial care. A disabling accident could also result in the need for non-skilled care, especially in the younger population. Non-skilled care normally lasts for a period of 100 days to several years. This describes *true* long-term care. Unlike short-term care received for a condition from which a person will recuperate, custodial care is not covered by regular health insurance or Medicare.

THE CONTINUUM OF LONG-TERM CARE

Most people mistakenly view "long-term care" as synonymous with "nursing home care." The reality is that a person's care normally progresses through a continuum of care that may never require nursing home confinement. For example, older people experiencing the frailties of aging may first require only a minimal amount of assistance in their home for a few hours each week. If the condition worsens and they experience problems with maintaining their balance, taking medications, or loss of memory, a move to an assisted living community may be the next step on the continuum of care.

Unless the condition worsens, or a terminal illness develops, the need for more comprehensive care in a nursing home will probably never be required. This trend toward helping people avoid nursing home care and receive care in a more comfortable setting is a bright spot in the generally somber subject of long-term care.

The myth that a need for long-term care automatically means a nursing home confinement exists because at one time, nursing homes were the first, last and ONLY option available for people who needed care and could no longer live at home. Now, nursing homes are just one of many environments in an expanding continuum of long-term care. In fact, due to the more positive preferences of home care and assisted living communities, nursing homes are now utilized less often for *true* long-term care delivery—a trend that is expected to continue.

As our population continues to age, it's anticipated that delivery systems unknown today will become common tomorrow. Not only will this have the obvious effect of providing the most appropriate level of services, it will also encourage people to become more comfortable with facing this difficult issue of planning ahead for long-term care.

THE VARIOUS LONG-TERM CARE SETTINGS
The Family Home

Most people who need care prefer to remain in familiar surroundings for as long as possible. The preferred environment for receiving long-term care is and always has been the family home, which is where the continuum of care begins. Currently, over 10 million people receive care at home, and home care is projected to increase 178% by 2030.

Although the lower cost of home care is an obvious factor in the decision to receive care at home, most people who can afford to pay for institutional care will still remain at home for as long as possible. According to the *National Long-Term Care Survey,* 57% of all people with a disability rely exclusively on unpaid care from family members or other informal caregivers at home. "Even among people who need assistance with up to five activities of daily living, about 41% relied entirely on unpaid care [at home]."

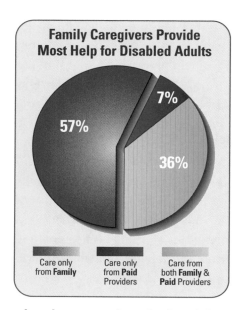

Family Caregivers Provide Most Help for Disabled Adults

7%

57%

36%

Care only from **Family**

Care only from **Paid** Providers

Care from both **Family** & **Paid** Providers

Medical advances and training have made home care even more practical by allowing home care providers to administer an ever-expanding array of services in a person's own home. The home care industry is a multibillion-dollar industry and exists to support this preferable environment for long-term care services.

When seeking home care services, as with all other long-term care services, the most satisfied consumers are those who do research, ask the right questions, and shop for quality providers. The Joint Commission on Accreditation of Healthcare Organizations has a good list of questions to ask home health care providers. This information is available on the web at **www.jcaho.org** or call the Joint Commission at 1-630-792-5800.

Services commonly available as a part of home care include:

- **Health Care** — nursing, physical and other rehabilitative services, help with medications, monitoring, and medical equipment
- **Personal Care** — assistance with personal hygiene, dressing, getting in and out of bed, bathing, and exercise
- **Nutrition** — meal planning, cooking, meal delivery, or meals at outside community sites
- **Homemaking** — housekeeping, shopping, home repair services, and household paperwork
- **Social and Safety** — escort and transportation services, companions, and coordination of provider services

Not surprisingly, the home care benefit of an LTC insurance policy has been cited as one of the most important reasons for owning LTC insurance. Home care benefits allow family members and friends to remain more involved in the emotional well-being of the policyholder's care, relieving the family from performing the exhausting physical caregiving tasks.

When family members are given a choice of whether or not to help with physical care, positive results occur. Studies have shown that even with paid help, friends and family members continue to provide some of the physical aspects of care. A study by the U.S. Department of Health and Human Services shows that family members still performed 40% of the care themselves, even when their loved one received care from paid providers. Two-thirds of the informal caregivers continued offering some level of care even with the presence of professional help. This study proves that formal care delivered by professionals does not completely replace the informal care provided by friends and family members.

This research suggests that people with the ability and determination to remain at home *and* who have the funds to hire supplemental help will get the best of both worlds: professional help plus the caring support of their loved ones. The ability to hire help greatly reduces the stress on family members and allows them to give more of the emotional care that is so often overlooked by a family caregiver who is overwhelmed with the physical tasks of care. "The two systems [formal and informal caregiving at home] work well together to better meet the needs of the entire family," the study concludes.

Adult Day Centers

Staying at home does not necessarily mean staying at home 24-hours-a-day. Adult day centers provide people with a safe, supportive, supervised place to stay during the day while their informal caregivers are at work or taking a much-needed respite.

There are almost 4,000 adult day centers in the United States. They provide care for 170,000 people each day, and this number will increase substantially as the population ages.

Adult day centers allow people to get out and interact socially, making them more likely to pay attention to their personal care, focus more on outside events and spend less time focusing on their disabilities. This socializing aspect has proven to contribute in a positive way to the overall health of the individual in need. Studies

Adult Day Centers

- Nearly **78%** of adult day centers are operated on a nonprofit or public basis.

- **74%** of adult day centers are affiliated with larger organizations such as home care, skilled nursing facilities, medical centers, or multi-purpose senior organizations.

- The average age of the adult day center participant is 72; two-thirds are women.

- **50%** of the participants using adult day centers nationwide have some cognitive impairment; one-third require nursing services at least weekly.

- **59%** of the participants require assistance with two or more activities of daily living. **41%** require assistance with three or more activities of daily living.

National Adult Day Services Association

have shown that adult day centers may actually help people stay at home longer.

Most adult day centers provide well-balanced meals and a variety of recreational activities. Many centers can accommodate people with relatively severe disabilities. Some even offer preventative health services and therapeutic activities.

The National Adult Day Services Association is a non-profit association that can help you locate adult day services in your area. Additional information can be found on their website at **www.nadsa.org** or by calling 1-866-890-7357.

Senior Centers

Senior centers are defined as places where "older adults can come together for services and activities that reflect their experience and skills, respond to their diverse needs and interests, enhance their dignity and support their independence" (National Council on Aging, **www.ncoa.org/content**). Several research studies have found that participation in senior center activities has a positive impact on feelings of self-worth and individual growth. Originally intended for social interaction, they are now becoming more comprehensive with a new emphasis on service and community involvement. As a sign of the times, many are adding new services such as training in computer skills.

There are now 16,000 senior centers across the country. They serve approximately 11 million older adults every year. Services are funded in part by the Older Americans Act, the YMCA, and the United Way.

Multipurpose Senior Centers are a gateway to the National Aging Services Network, which includes more than 30,000 local, regional, tribal, and national service providers for older adults and their caregivers. These centers are often the source of vital community-based social and nutritional support, allowing older Americans to remain independent. But, their objective is to serve both active and frail elders.

Typical services include:
- Health and wellness programs
- Meals and nutrition
- Education in arts and humanities
- Intergenerational programs
- Employment assistance
- Community action and volunteer opportunities
- Transportation
- Leisure travel
- Financial assistance
- Information and referrals

By using a combination of adult day centers and the services provided by senior centers, thousands of people are able to significantly extend the time they are able to stay in their home environment. But if a person's health declines and the management of day-to-day care becomes more complicated, remaining at home may become difficult and costly. At this point on the continuum of care, some other type of residential care environment may become a more realistic option.

Board and Care Homes

For a home-like environment, care provided by familiar faces, and relatively low cost, board and care homes can be a good solution for people who need simple assistance, such as help with meal preparation, medication monitoring, and personal care.

Board and care homes are private dwellings where a family or group provides care for a limited number of people with disabilities. The typical number of residents is two to ten. Some converted single-family dwellings are allowed only five or six residents.

A board and care home may offer residents the services found in an assisted living community, a skilled nursing home or in some cases, an Alzheimer's facility. Generally, however, most board and care homes do not offer skilled nursing or medical services, and are not the solution for severely disabled people. But they can provide a safe, supportive environment for people who want to actively make choices about daily life and health care and maintain as much independence as possible.

Some board and care homes serve the needs of those with similar conditions. For example, some specialize in care for people in the middle to late stages of Alzheimer's. Others may only care for early-stage Alzheimer's patients. Some may only be licensed to care for those who have mild mental impairment, or assist those who need relatively minor help (reminders, meal service, laundry, housekeeping help, and driving services).

Since the federal government does not certify board and care homes, the quality of care provided in care homes can vary widely. In some areas, the local government may enforce only minimal regulations with periodic inspections for compliance. Therefore, it's important to find someone you trust to help you with the decision to place a loved one in a board and care home. For example, have family members, a lawyer, and a financial professional review contracts before entering into an agreement or paying an entrance fee.

Also, do some research on the home including:
- Checking for complaints with the state licensing agency
- Asking for and checking references
- Making unscheduled, unannounced visits at different hours
- Checking the website: **www.seniorresource.com**

Assisted Living Communities

The most common long-term care delivery system for the first two decades of the 21st century will be assisted living communities. Assisted living is the fastest growing type of care setting because it meets the needs of people who cannot make it entirely on their own, but do not need or want the skilled nursing care and institutional environment of a nursing home. In contrast to nursing homes, typically viewed as the place where "old folks go to die," assisted living communities are a relatively recent and promising phenomenon.

The Assisted Living Federation of America defines an assisted living residence as "a combination of housing, personalized support services, and health care, designed to meet the needs—both scheduled and unscheduled—of those who need help with the activities of daily living." This association can provide you with an extensive consumer checklist for choosing an assisted living community. See their website at: **www.alfa.org**.

A major benefit of the assisted living option is the relief from stress experienced by family members who often find caring for a loved one at home extremely difficult as the loved one's health declines. Choosing to move into assisted living generally means that although you need assistance, you still value your independence and want to remain in a home-like environment. Assisted living offers a philosophy of care that emphasizes values such as individuality, privacy, and choice.

A typical resident in assisted living is a person in their 70s or 80s. Common health problems of residents include Alzheimer's, slight memory loss, incontinence, and loss of mobility.

Over 1 million Americans live in the 39,105 assisted living communities throughout the country. The demand for assisted living services resulted in a 61% increase in the number of communities built from 1998 through 2006.

Assisted living communities typically offer the following services:

- Health promotion and exercise programs
- Social and recreational services
- Three meals a day in a common dining area
- Housekeeping services
- Transportation
- Assistance with such activities as eating, bathing, dressing, and toileting
- Access to health and medical services
- 24-hour security and staff
- Emergency call systems in each room
- Medication management

Philosophy of Care in Assisted Living

- Offering cost-effective quality care that is personalized for individual needs.
- Fostering independence for each resident.
- Treating each resident with dignity and respect.
- Promoting the individuality of each resident.
- Allowing each resident choice of care and lifestyle.
- Protecting each resident's right to privacy.
- Nurturing the spirit of each resident.
- Involving family and friends.
- Providing a safe, residential environment.
- Making the assisted living residence a valuable community asset.

www.alfa.org/public/articles

The term "assisted living" covers a variety of settings, which can range from remodeled Victorians to high-rise apartments. The typical assisted living residence has from 25 to 120 units, which may vary in size from single rooms to full-size apartments. Accommodations cover the spectrum from luxurious to spartan, with fees to match.

The cost of care in assisted living communities is less than the cost of nursing homes and, in many cases, can be more economical than home care. For example, assisted living care for a patient with Alzheimer's is 19% less than the same care provided at home.

Assisted living is paid for with private dollars. Residents or their families normally pay the bill out of pocket. One alternative to paying for care with accumulated savings or assets is LTC insurance—discussed in detail in later chapters. Although LTC insurance is a relatively new type of insurance, 2.1% of residents in assisted living communities are already paying for care by collecting on their LTC insurance policy.

People in assisted living usually have fewer ADL limitations than those in nursing homes. Nursing home residents use more medical services, skilled nursing care, nutritional services, and social services than assisted living residents. Assisted living residents are much more likely to receive health care services from their private physicians, utilizing transportation services available through the community.

People living in assisted living are about twice as likely as nursing home residents to assess their health as average or good. Often the difference is one of attitude, and does not necessarily correlate with the clinical diagnosis or true health of residents. Many people in assisted living simply feel more positive about themselves and their health than those in nursing homes.

Continuing Care Retirement Communities

Continuing Care Retirement Communities (CCRC's) have an awkward name, and a high price tag. But they can offer an excellent approach to aging-in-place for those who can afford the fees. The reasoning behind CCRC's is that people will naturally require higher levels of care and support as they age. Therefore, it makes sense to accommodate the full spectrum of needs on the same campus and within the same community.

CCRC's offer assisted living units, which are normally available in the form of small studio or one-bedroom apartments with scaled-down kitchens. Group dining rooms and common areas for socializing and recreation are often available. A resident may begin their stay in an apartment designed for active, independent living. If their health declines, they may move into assisted living in the same community. If their health continues to decline, the community may offer skilled nursing facilities. If the resident recovers, or if their health improves, they can easily move back to a lower level of care.

This continuum of care makes a great deal of sense and provides the peace of mind of knowing where you'll be and how you'll receive care regardless of any changes in your health.

Some of the services typically offered in a CCRC include:

- Nursing and other skilled medical care
- Assisted living
- Personal assistance
- Emergency help
- Meals, including special diet needs
- Housekeeping
- Scheduled transportation
- Recreational, educational, and social activities

If cost were no object, CCRC's, rather than assisted living communities, would be the wave of the future for long-term care delivery. Cost, however, is very much an issue and the price of CCRC's is well beyond the means of many people. According to the American Association of Retired Persons (AARP), the up-front entrance fees for CCRC's range from $20,000 to $400,000. Once you pay that lump sum, you still face monthly rent and fees that rival the costs of assisted living communities. But for those with sufficient means, moving into a CCRC can be a permanent solution to a potential need for long-term care, eliminating the stress and uncertainty of how you'll be cared for in the future.

A resident of a CCRC signs a long-term (normally lifetime) contract when he or she moves on the campus. The contract is a legal agreement between the resident and the community. You should familiarize yourself with the following three common types of contracts if you are considering this option. The type of contract you agree to will determine the level of service you will receive.

- **Extensive Contracts** — The most expensive option, extensive contracts offer unlimited long-term care for little or no increase in the normal monthly payments.

- **Modified Contracts** — A middle-of-the-road approach, modified contracts provide care for a specified length of time (usually three to five years). Beyond the specified limit, you're responsible for your own costs.

- **Fee-For-Service** — An agreement that reduces up-front payments but exposes you to potential high costs in the future. Fee-for-service contracts specify that you pay the full rate for all long-term care services you require.

CCRC's sometimes have a group LTC insurance policy, which a resident is required to purchase when entering the community. If you are considering moving into a CCRC in the near future, ask the CCRC about their LTC insurance purchase requirement before you purchase private LTC insurance. Some facilities include LTC insurance as part of their payment fees. If this is the case, you may not need private LTC insurance.

If you already own LTC insurance, ask the facility administrator if the CCRC will waive the requirement to purchase their coverage. If the CCRC will not waive the requirement to purchase their group coverage, consult your financial advisor prior to canceling your private coverage.

The American Association of Homes and Services for the Aging (AAHSA) provides a consumer directory and additional information about CCRC's on their website at **www.aahsa.org** or call 1-202-783-2242. The Continuing Care Accreditation Commission (CCAC) at **www.ccaconline.org** lists all communities that have met specific standards of certification.

Alzheimer's Facilities

Alzheimer's Disease now afflicts approximately 4.5 million Americans, and impacts another 19 million who have a family member with the disease. By 2025, these figures are projected to grow by 75%.

According to a report published in November 2001, individuals who suffer from Alzheimer's Disease can require care for 8 years or longer, the longest average duration of long-term care services (U.S. Department of Labor 2001). Finding and receiving specialized care can be difficult because people with Alzheimer's Disease have a different set of needs than those with simpler "age-related" health conditions. In addition to assistance with ADLs, they require ongoing social stimulation and close supervision.

Alzheimer's facilities can offer a good choice for care. These facilities are specifically designed with smaller spaces to accommodate multiple activities. The hallways are designed in a circular fashion, and in many cases, the resident's doors are color-coded. Other than specialized services and the design of the facilities, Alzheimer's facilities are very similar in most ways to assisted living communities.

The Alzheimer's Association (**www.alz.org** or 1-800-272-3900) offers additional information about living options for those with Alzheimer's and support services for their families.

Nursing Homes

Nursing homes are the last stop on the continuum of long-term care. They offer a necessary and important role in long-term care and the continuum of care would not be complete without them.

About 1.6 million people age 65 and older live in nursing homes. The average age of residents is 82 years old with women making up the majority of residents.

We place nursing homes last on the continuum of care because:

- Most people will only go into a nursing home as a last resort,

  and

- By planning ahead for long-term care, it's very unlikely that you will need to enter a nursing home for an extended period of time.

Nursing homes are by far the most institutional setting in the delivery-of-care spectrum. They are designed to provide mostly medical care to severely physically and cognitively disabled patients during their declining months or years. A variety of studies have shown that elderly patients who spend longer than two years in a nursing facility rarely return home.

Unlike all the other types of care explained above, a physician must certify a resident's need for nursing home care. The physician must visit regularly and assume responsibility for the patient's over-all treatment of care.

As with any type of long-term care services, the quality of care can vary widely from one nursing home to the next. Unfortunately, the quality of care provided will be determined mostly by our ability to pay for our care. Nursing homes, like any business, must cover their operating costs. This isn't easy with the monies received from Medicaid reimbursements—especially for nursing homes that have high-quality services available *(for more on Medicaid see Chapter 4: Who Pays for Long-Term Care?)*. As a result, many nursing homes limit the number of beds available for welfare patients.

Private pay patients are assured "bed availability" and quality care in the facility of their choice. By planning ahead long before there is a need for care, you and your family will have more control over your long-term care delivery options and the quality of care you receive.

The American Health Care Association is a good resource for information about nursing homes (202-842-4444, **www.ahca.org**).

Auntie Mae "Blossoms" in Assisted Living

Auntie Mae is the perfect example of the typical resident in assisted living. A widow in her 80s, she had lived alone for many years, supporting herself by taking on work as a seamstress. During a visit, I noticed that she was behaving "strangely," almost as if she were having hallucinations. After a visit to the doctor and a subsequent review of her medications, it was determined that Auntie Mae had been taking too much medication. We attempted to organize her medications and schedule so that she wouldn't forget she had already taken the medication and "double-dose." But without someone to remind her, she'd forget to use the reminder system and was once again found in a drug-induced fog.

At this point it was clear that Auntie Mae could no longer live by herself. Since she only needed limited assistance and was intent on maintaining her independence, with no desire to move in with her children, assisted living offered the perfect alternative. She now lives in a community that provides her with her own personal unit with a bedroom, bath, and a small living room and kitchenette. She hasn't had any further incidents of over medicating herself: the staff members monitor her schedule. In addition, we've found that the social activities available to her have made her "blossom" and enjoy life again. Both her physical and mental health have improved significantly with this new living arrangement.

— *Kathleen Deknis*

KEY POINTS

Where is Long-Term Care Received?

➤ *Skilled care* is provided when intensive medical attention is required. Medicare and most private insurance plans cover Skilled care.

➤ *Non-skilled care,* also known as *Custodial care* is provided when the prognosis is progressive deterioration over a long period of time (100 days or longer) with little chance of recovery. Custodial care is never covered by Medicare, Medicare Supplement insurance, or private health insurance.

The Continuum of Long-Term Care includes all the settings in which long-term care services are received:

➤ The **family home** remains the preferred environment for receiving long-term care.

➤ **Board and care homes** are private dwellings that offer care in a home-like environment for a limited number of people who need minor assistance.

➤ **Assisted living communities** provide personal assistance and low-level nursing care—all on the same campus.

➤ **Continuing Care Retirement Communities** offer facilities ranging from apartments for independent and active residents, to assisted living arrangements, and, in some cases, skilled nursing care.

➤ **Alzheimer's facilities** offer unique floorplans and provide the special care needed by people who have been diagnosed with Alzheimer's Disease.

➤ **Nursing Homes** provide mostly medical care to severely physically and cognitively disabled patients during their declining months or years.

Chapter 3

How Much Does Long-Term Care Cost?

*The future, according to some scientists,
will be exactly like the past, only far more expensive.*

— John Sladde, *Science Fiction Writer (1937-2000)*

Senator John Heinz was one of the first to understand the need to have a plan for long-term care. He understood that if you made a list of potential "big ticket items," you probably wouldn't think to include long-term care. Yet, long-term care expenses may cost more during your lifetime than any other single expenditure.

Specific costs of long-term care services vary widely. **The three major factors that drive the cost of long-term care are:**

> The greatest threat to the financial security of Americans is the cost of long-term care. (We) can insure our cars against theft or damage, our houses against flood, fire and earthquakes, our children against the costs of college and braces, and our families against the risks of an early death. But when it comes to insuring our single greatest threat to our life savings and emotional reserves, the costs of long-term care, Americans have no (plan). In many ways, it's as if we are all wearing bulletproof vests with holes over our hearts.
>
> *(paraphrased)*
> The late Senator John Heinz,
> *Select Committee on Aging*

1. **Geographic location:** As with all living expenses, the cost will largely depend on the part of the country where the care is received.

2. **The place in which the care is received:** The various environments, the levels of care, and the continuum of care were explained in *Chapter 2.*

3. **Reason(s) for care:** The severity of the condition causing the need for care can vary the costs by thousands of dollars per month.

The statistics and costs given in this chapter represent national averages for care received in various settings. The specific costs of care in your area can be obtained from a financial advisor who utilizes the *Comprehensive Planning Approach* to long-term care.

FAST FACTS:

- Depending on the severity of the need for care, home care can be the most expensive or the least expensive option.

- **88%** of people 50 and older will receive help from family members and other informal caregivers at some time during their lifetime. For people with long-term care insurance, that figure is **40%**.

- Women account for **75%** of caregivers 50 and older.

- Among caregivers aged 50–64, **60%** must juggle full- or part-time work *and* caregiving.

- **58%** of caregivers must make changes in their work schedules to provide care.

- **19%** of caregivers report physical or mental health problems as a result of caregiving.

GEOGRAPHIC LOCATION AND ENVIRONMENT

Home Care

The national average rate for a nurse to come to your home is $43 per hour. The average rate for a non-skilled person to come to your home is $23 per hour.

But, in expensive areas of the country, a visit from a Licensed Practical Nurse can cost over $100 per hour. Even unskilled services can cost more than $35 per hour.

Home care also involves services beyond personnel. When you add up all the average expenses for home care, including personnel, medical equipment, and supplies, the total cost for home care on a daily basis averages $92.

Assisted Living Communities

Assisted living communities will provide most long-term care services for at least the next 2 decades. They offer a more pleasant and positive living environment at a lower cost than nursing homes.

Most assisted living communities charge by the month. The average national cost of care per month is $2,640. But the costs can vary from a low of $1,800 per month to a high of $6,300 per month or more.

These figures do not include any care received beyond assistance with two activities of daily living. People who need care above and beyond this basic level of care will incur additional costs. Still, compared to nursing home care and, in some instances, home care, assisted living communities offer one of the best values in long-term care delivery.

Nursing Homes

The national average daily rate for nursing home care is $206 for a private room. The cost for a semi-private room is $188 per day. That comes to an average *annual* cost of over $75,000 for a private room, and over $68,000 for semi-private accommodations.

But the actual cost of care in a nursing home varies almost as widely as home care and is mainly influenced by city and region. For example, in Orlando, a private room is a relative bargain at $108 per day, compared to high-cost cities such as Boston at $261 per day, and San Francisco at $290 per day.

Although these are the documented figures, these "average" costs of nursing home care may be on the low side. Medicaid, the welfare program, pays for nursing home care for those who are impoverished. Analysts point out that most nursing homes lose money on Medicaid patients, because they must accept Medicaid's low reimbursement rates. This results in Medicaid services being delivered at less than true market value. These low reimbursement payments are included in the averaging of nursing home costs, and thus may distort the true average cost of nursing home care. *(For a more detailed explanation of Medicaid, see Chapter 4.)*

REASON(S) FOR CARE

In addition to your geographic location and the environment in which long-term care is received, the reason(s) long-term care is needed has a major impact on the costs. Some long-term care services, such as minor assistance with ADLs, can be relatively inexpensive. Specialized types of care, such as services provided to people with Alzheimer's Disease, are expensive by comparison. In fact, the average amount spent over a lifetime of long-term care for an Alzheimer's patient is $204,000, making it the third most expensive disease in the United States, behind heart disease and cancer.

THE IMPORTANCE OF CONSIDERING INFLATION

In developing a plan for long-term care, the most relevant figures are not the costs of care today but the projection of costs, taking into consideration the effects of inflation. Once your plan is developed, it's wise to consult with your LTC Planning expert at least annually, to review the plan and make sure it considers the newly inflated costs of care.

The rate of inflation for long-term care expenses has remained at a reasonable level in recent years. This trend is predicted to continue due to the surge in availability of reasonably priced assisted living communities. Specifically, expenses are predicted to rise at an annual rate of between 4% and 7% between now and 2015.

But the demand for long-term care services—due to baby boomers moving into their 70s and 80s—could result in long-term care inflation rates approaching double digits after 2015. It's imperative that you stay aware of the actual inflation rates in future years, so that your plan for long-term care accomplishes its objectives.

IMPACT OF FAMILY CAREGIVING ON CAREERS

40%   Unable to advance in careers

75%   Affects their health

66%   Affects their lifetime earnings

96%   Make informal workplace adjustments

84%   Make formal workplace adjustments

THE SILENT COSTS OF LONG-TERM CARE

The costs of care from a line-item standpoint do not tell the entire story. The physical, emotional, and psychological impact to caregivers providing care, as well as lost income opportunities, must also be included in any discussion pertaining to the true costs of long-term care.

Family Care: The Loss in Income and Assets

Most caregivers are family members who attempt to maintain their careers while caring for a loved one. Over half of those providing care are employed full-time, while another 13% work part-time.

We usually think of family caregivers as providing care "free of charge", but the fact is that those who balance caregiving and employment pay a heavy price for their caregiving responsibilities. Although most family caregivers begin by simply providing occasional assistance to a relative or spouse, many families providing care eventually alter their lifestyle and career choices.

In a series of surveys called *"The Juggling Act Study,"* MetLife attempted to measure the financial consequences to families who balance caregiving with work. A large majority of family caregivers reported the need for flexible hours—to arrive at work late or leave early—and to take time off during the day. They also had to use sick leave and vacation time to meet caregiving obligations. Family caregivers reported other common strategies to juggle career and caregiving, including decreasing work hours, taking a leave of absence, switching to part-time work, quitting entirely, or taking early retirement.

By measuring the "cumulative effects from wage reductions, lost retirement and pension benefits, compromised opportunities for training/promotion, and stress-related health problems," the study found that family caregivers sacrifice an astonishing amount of earning potential. "The average total financial loss as a result of caregiving by a family member is estimated at $659,139 over the lifetime (of the caregiver)."

Family Caregivers: Physical & Emotional Burdens

In considering the role of caregiver, it's important to measure the physical and emotional exhaustion that might be experienced by a caregiver trying to care for a full-sized adult—in some cases twice the size of the caregiver. Consider the physical and emotional aspect when planning for long-term care for your family by asking yourself:

- Will I be able to help him/her transfer in and out of bed? On and off the toilet?

- Will I be able to roll him/her over in bed to change clothing and bedding?

- Will I be able to help him/her bathe or shower?

- Will I be able to get him/her dressed and undressed?

- Will I feel comfortable providing personal care and hygiene for him/her?

The Average Length of Family Caregiving

Most family members who provide care never anticipated becoming a caregiver. For those who did consider becoming a caregiver, few accurately anticipated the number of hours per week they would eventually devote to caregiving, or the months or years the care would be needed. The majority of participants in the survey estimated they would need to provide care from six months to two years. The actual average length of family caregiving is eight years!

Given the stress and time pressures they faced, it's no surprise that three-quarters of participants reported that caregiving had adversely affected their own health. More than 20% experienced a significant decline in health, and an increase in the number of visits to their own healthcare providers.

The Sandwich Generation: Time, Energy, and Money Spread Thin Between Elderly and Children

A growing challenge for many families is the recently coined category called the "sandwich generation": people who are caught in the middle of caring for an older relative while still raising their children.

The financial, physical, and emotional burdens of caregiving while at the same time raising children, has a severely negative impact on these families. The time and attention once given to children and spouse is diverted to an ailing parent. The physical energy of the caregiver depletes as they strive to juggle their caregiving duties with maintaining a healthy family life. The time and money they once accrued for family vacations may now be used to supplement the care and services needed by the ill family member.

The costs associated with caregiving are not merely computed in dollar figures. The costs all too often are defined in terms of strained relationships with a spouse, behavioral problems manifested in children, and the emotional and/or physical breakdown of the caregiver as a result of spreading him/herself too thin. These costs are the additional silent costs—costs *in addition* to the direct financial costs of long-term care.

Grandmother Changed "Overnight"

My husband's grandmother was always meticulous about her housekeeping and was an impeccable dresser. We were naturally shocked when my husband went to take her to lunch one day and found her still in her robe, looking confused, and the house in disarray. He knew something was terribly wrong and immediately called his mother. An appointment was arranged for her to be evaluated by her doctor. Her doctor's assessment, followed by subsequent testing, confirmed that she was in the early stages of dementia.

The family decided that it was no longer safe for her to live alone and moved her into an assisted living community close by. The cost of care at that time was $2,000 per month. After several years, she was diagnosed with Alzheimer's and required more care than the assisted living community could provide. She was eventually moved into a nursing home. She passed away 14 years later. While settling her affairs, we made the last monthly payment to the nursing home: **$12,000!**

— *Ruth Simpson*

KEY POINTS

How Much Does Long-Term Care Cost?

➤ The factors that determine the costs of long-term care are geographic location, environment where care is received, and the severity of the person's condition.

➤ Assisted Living Communities charge by the month and costs can vary from a low of $1,800/month to a high of $6,300/month or more.

➤ The average annual cost in a nursing home is over $75,000 for a private room and over $68,000 for a semi-private room.

➤ The predicted average annual rate of inflation for long-term care in the next few years is between 4% and 7%. Beyond approximately 2015, double-digit inflation is likely, due to the need for long-term care by aging baby boomers.

➤ The average total financial loss as a result of caregiving by a family member is estimated to be $659,139 over the lifetime of the caregiver.

➤ The silent costs of caregiving by family members include an impact on current lifestyle and career goals, postponement of retirement, stress-related health problems, and strained relationships.

➤ The phrase "sandwich generation" is often used to define people caught in the middle of caring for an older relative(s) while still raising children.

Chapter 4 — Who Pays for Long-Term Care?

*We have not passed that subtle line
between childhood and adulthood until...
we have stopped saying "It got lost"
and start saying "I lost it."*

— Sidney J. Harris

Sources of funding for long-term care expenses are a major concern for our state and federal governments because long-term care expenditures could expand to the point of dwarfing our current "health care crisis." Increases in life expectancy, the size of the baby boom generation, and inflation of health care costs are driving this expensive problem.

With the help of financial advisors, government analysts, and experts on aging, Americans are beginning to understand that long-term care expenses could represent their greatest risk to financial security. Due to the new awareness of this financial and emotional risk, many Americans are taking action by making deliberate plans to protect their families and their legacy against the impact of long-term care.

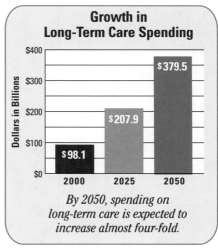

Growth in Long-Term Care Spending

By 2050, spending on long-term care is expected to increase almost four-fold.

But most Americans are still confused about who pays for long-term care. While services for physician and hospital care are covered by Medicare and regular health insurance, sources for payment of long-term care expenses are limited.

FAST FACTS:
WHAT WE DON'T KNOW CAN HURT US

- **71%** of Medicare recipients mistakenly believe Medicare is a primary source for covering long-term care.

- Most people mistakenly believe a Medicare Supplement policy will pay for long-term care.

- **87%** of people under age 65 mistakenly believe their private health insurance will cover the cost of long-term care.

There are four sources for providing or paying for long-term care:

1. Family
2. Medicaid (Medi-Cal in California), the welfare program
3. Personal assets
4. Long-term care insurance

Some of the pros and cons of these sources are explained below. Long-term care insurance is explained only briefly because an in-depth discussion of insurance is provided in future chapters.

At the end of this chapter, we dispel some myths about other sources normally believed to cover long-term care and provide you with a clearer understanding of what these programs actually do and don't cover.

FAMILY

When a loved one needed care in past decades, other family members took on the role of caregiver. Women, usually wives, daughters, and daughters-in-law, were the most likely providers of care for immediate and extended family members.

But changes have occurred in our society that make it less likely that our family will be in a position to provide our care. Families today are not only much smaller, but many are also spread across the globe, with two careers needed to support the family's financial obligations. Even relying on a spouse for care may not be an option due to changes in the traditional American family structure. In the future, *paid* caregivers will be the most common source for providing long-term care services.

As explained in *Chapter 3,* caring for a loved one is a necessity for many families who failed to deliberately plan for long-term care. According to a study conducted by the National Alliance for Caregivers, the number of U.S. households providing care to adults aged

50 and over has more than quadrupled in the past 13 years. The average caregiver is a married, middle class woman in her late 40s, caring for her mother-in-law, and/or her own mother, usually in that order. But 28% of caregivers are men. Over half of those providing care are employed full-time, and another 13 percent work part-time.

Some well-meaning children insist that they will personally provide for their parents' long-term care. This is contrary to the wishes of most parents, who will do almost anything to keep from becoming a burden on their children.

But if you decide that relying on your family *is* a viable option to use as your plan for care, talk seriously with your spouse and children about the type of care they can and will provide. This option is best evaluated with the advice of a financial professional, to assure that everyone's responsibilities are clearly outlined in writing. It may also be a good idea to have your family members present when developing the specifics of your plan: the need for care often has less impact on the person in need of care than it has on the rest of the family.

MEDICAID, THE WELFARE PROGRAM

Medicaid, the welfare program, provides funding for approximately 45% of all long-term care expenses in the United States. The Federal and State funded program began in 1965 for the purpose of providing medical care for impoverished, elderly, blind or disabled persons who could not afford the cost of care. The lack of other payment options, especially for nursing home care, has resulted in a large portion of nursing home residents relying solely on the Medicaid program to pay for their care.

Eligibility for Medicaid

Medicaid laws have been revised many times since the creation of the program. The result is a convoluted legal structure used to determine eligibility for Medicaid benefits. There are various "look-back periods" if you transfer assets, asset transfer penalties, income caps, and waiting periods.

Medicaid is a needs-based program and eligibility is determined by an evaluation of a person's assets and income. The rules are complex, vary between states, and are subject to change every year.

Although the federal government issues guidelines regarding benefits, each state is allowed to implement these guidelines according to their own interpretation. The Medicaid program varies so widely in the amount and duration of benefits, the United States has experienced a growing phenomenon called "Medicaid Migration": the act of moving from state to state in search of the most generous benefits. At present, the phenomenon is small, but it shows the seriousness of the long-term care dilemma.

Generally, eligibility for Medicaid requires that an applicant meet five tests:

1. ***Citizenship.*** A Medicaid long-term care beneficiary must be a U.S. citizen or a "qualified alien" (for example, a permanent resident, a refugee, an asylee or person granted conditional entry).

2. ***Residence.*** The applicant must be a resident of the state where the application is filed.

3. ***Medical Need.*** In order to qualify for long term-care assistance, the applicant must show a need for long-term care. Each state has its own method of making this determination. Typically, the applicant must show impairment with several "activities of daily living", such as eating, dressing, and bathing.

4. ***Resources.*** The applicant may not have more than the allowable amount of assets. But an asset is not simply an asset: it is exempt, non-exempt, available, or unavailable. What is considered exempt or unavailable varies from state to state but typically a single applicant may have no more than $2,000 in available assets, in addition to exempt assets such as their residence. There are special rules and exceptions for married couples, to guard against "spousal impoverishment". These rules and exceptions also vary from state to state.

5. ***Income.*** In "medically needy" states, income eligibility is met by having an income too low to cover the actual cost of care. However, nearly half of the states employ an "income cap" to determine whether an applicant qualifies for Medicaid. Individuals who meet the other requirements but whose income exceeds the cap will not be eligible.

Share of Cost

In "medically needy" states, where excess income does not trigger ineligibility, the state sets a "maintenance need standard", or an amount of the beneficiary's income that may be allocated to living expenses. Individuals whose monthly income is higher than this set limit must pay for their care with the difference between their income and the set maintenance need standard. Known as the "share of cost", this money is essentially a co-payment for medical and nursing home costs. The beneficiary is responsible for this share of cost before Medicaid will cover the remaining balance of the state's agreed upon cost of care each month. The amount a nursing home resident is allowed to retain after paying their share of cost is as low as $35.00 per month in some states.

Accessibility to Care

Medicaid licensed providers are reimbursed by the government, but the payment is less than the private pay rate. As a result, nursing homes that have a high number of Medicaid patients generate less income than non-Medicaid nursing homes. For this reason, a private paying patient will generally be given priority admission over a Medicaid patient. Medicaid recipients are sometimes placed on a waiting list to enter a facility, even if there are beds available. In the meantime, they must rely on other resources for care – resources that may be inadequate, further compromising their health. This practice is common because only a few states have enacted laws prohibiting admission practices based on the source of payment.

For most people in need of long-term care, receiving care at home or in an assisted living environment is emotionally preferable to moving into a nursing home. But in general, the choices for high quality care at home or in assisted living are reserved for private pay patients.

Quality-of-Care Issues

There is an ongoing debate regarding the difference between the quality of care received by Medicaid beneficiaries and care received by private pay patients. For example, my wife's grandmother paid for her long-term care services with her own money until she became impoverished, and was forced to rely on welfare. The quality of care she received while she was "private pay" was noticeably superior to the care she received once she was on welfare. *(See "When the Money Under the Mattress is Gone" at the end of the chapter.)*

Evidence that there may be a quality of care deficency for Medicaid patients was brought to light in November of 2001 by the ERISA (Employee Retirement Income Security Act) Advisory Council with the statement, "Medicaid reimbursement rates are so low that they may compromise quality of care, as well as the financial viability of the long-term care industry."

Medicaid Planning

Medicaid Planning is the process of positioning your income and assets so that you can legally qualify for Medicaid. Despite stories of "millionaires on Medicaid", the vast majority of people who enlist professional assistance with Medicaid Planning are not wealthy. Because of the quality of care deficiencies with Medicaid, it would be foolish for individuals who can afford private pay care to divest themselves of their assets for the purpose of receiving government paid care.

Medicaid Planning may be the only option for some people. For example, some people have a health condition and will not qualify for long-term care insurance. A person in this situation must consider using one of the remaining resources for paying for care.

The process of Medicaid Planning has a bad reputation because some unscrupulous practitioners have abused the system and taken unfair advantage of taxpayers. This is because there is no uniform regulation for companies or individuals who call themselves Medicaid Planners. Beware of practitioners who offer Medicaid Planning, but with the true purpose of exposing your assets for the purpose of selling financial products that may or may not be appropriate for your situation. The most ethical planners are licensed attorneys who are regulated by their state bar associations, and who utilize a process that professionally guides you through the myriad of complicated Medicaid rules. When considering Medicaid Planning, interview several Medicaid Planners, and use the services of a licensed attorney who utilizes the *Comprehensive Planning Approach* to long-term care.

Estate Recovery

A program called **Estate Recovery** reimburses the government for money spent by Medicaid for a beneficiary's care. The money is recovered from a deceased Medicaid beneficiary's estate. States' efforts to recapture this money are becoming more aggressive, closing any loopholes that allow a Medicaid beneficiary to leave money to family members until the government is reimbursed. Estate Recovery is now a required process in every state.

The Future of Medicaid

The Medicaid program is a lifesaver for some people needing care. But the ongoing expansion of the program has strained our government's budget. The availability of government funding for long-term care through Medicaid is likely to decrease sharply in the decades ahead. For baby-boomers and their children, planning ahead for a time when Medicaid will not be readily available is the wisest decision they can make for securing quality and affordable care.

In 2006, Congress passed the Deficit Reduction Act. This legislation will have profound implications to Medicaid and Medicaid Planning. For more information, read Stephen Moses' interview in Chapter 19 and ask your financial planner, estate planning attorney, or Certified Public Accountant (CPA) for more clarification.

PERSONAL ASSETS

Although people rarely make a deliberate decision to pay for care with their own money, Americans spend billions of dollars in personal assets annually on long-term care expenses. The dollar value of personal assets used to pay for care is predicted to double between 2007 and 2011. Personal assets used to pay for care are normally withdrawn from one or more of three places: personal savings, retirement accounts, and home equity.

When considering this option, analyze:

- Your ability to accumulate enough assets to pay for long-term care expenses.

- The impact on your family of risking your assets. Even if you can accumulate the necessary funds to pay for your care, a long-term care event will likely affect the current standard of living of your family. It could also compromise your legacy and deplete assets you and your family had hoped to leave to your heirs.

If you *do* choose the option of relying on your personal assets, having a written plan for long-term care will alleviate any surprises. Make sure the plan deliberately identifies and earmarks the exact funds you wish to be used to pay for your care.

LONG-TERM CARE INSURANCE

Long-term care insurance is specifically designed to cover long-term care expenses. Insurance can pay for care in a nursing home, assisted living community, at home, or in an adult day center.

Only about 4% of the population owns coverage, because this type of insurance has only been available for two decades. But as Americans become more knowledgeable about the need to plan ahead, LTC insurance is expected to become a major payer of long-term care expenses: By 2025, it's predicted that LTC insurance will pay a larger share of long-term care expenses than any other source, other than welfare.

We devote several chapters to a complete discussion of LTC insurance.

WHO PAYS FOR WHAT TYPES OF CARE?

	Reliance on Family	Welfare	Personal Assets	LTC Insurance
Home Care	?	Limited	Yes	Yes
Community Based Services	?	No	Yes	Yes
Adult Day Center	?	No	Yes	Yes
Assisted Living	?	No	Yes	Yes
Continuing Care Retirement Communities	?	No for Independent and Assisted; Limited for other care	Yes	No for Independent Living; Yes for all other care
Hospital Care	?	Yes	Yes	No
Skilled Nursing Home	?	Yes	Yes	Yes
Non-Skilled Nursing Home	?	Yes	Yes	Yes

MYTH: OTHER RESOURCES WILL PAY FOR LONG-TERM CARE

Most families are as shocked as we were when my grandfather needed care: we suddenly learned that Medicare and Medicare Supplement policies do not pay for long-term care expenses. Private health insurance plans also specifically *exclude* coverage for long-term care.

Medicare

Medicare provides health insurance coverage to Americans over age 65 and to some people with disabilities who are under age 65. Studies have shown that 71% of Medicare recipients believe Medicare is a primary source for paying for long-term care. But Medicare was enacted as a benefit to pay for physician and hospital care, and does not cover the expenses associated with the care of people who simply need assistance with activities of daily living or supervision due to cognitive impairment.

The myth regarding Medicare coverage for long-term care is caused by the wording in the *Medicare Handbook (U.S. Health and Human Services 2007)*. The handbook explains that, under certain conditions, Medicare covers the first 20 days in a skilled nursing home and another 80 days of care on a co-payment basis. But care with a duration of less than 100 days is *short-term care*.

Medicare's "short-term care" benefit is designed to partially cover rehabilitation from a serious injury or illness. A three-day prior hospitalization is required to qualify for benefits and care must be provided in an approved *skilled* nursing home. Custodial care, the most common level of care, is not covered by Medicare.

Private Benefits

■ **Medicare Supplement Insurance**

Medicare Supplement policies only cover services **approved** by Medicare. These policies do not cover long-term care.

Medicare Supplement policies may supplement short-term care. Specifically, Medicare Supplement coverage may offer a co-payment benefit for care provided by approved providers, beginning on the 21st day, and for up to 100 days of care in an approved *skilled* nursing home. This skilled care must also be preceded by a three-day hospitalization.

■ **Health Insurance**

Health insurance, like Medicare, is a provider of only "short-term care." Health care benefits cover most Americans against illness and accidents, but specifically exclude long-term care coverage. The maximum benefit for care provided by health insurance plans is 100 days.

When the Money Under the Mattress is Gone

Having lived through the great depression of the 1930s, Nana and Gramps lived very frugally on my grandfather's salary as a construction worker. As a result of careful planning, after Gramps passed away my grandmother was able to live comfortably on the money they had stashed away under the mattress (literally!).

When Nana first went into a nursing home, she went as a "private pay" patient. Allen and I were very impressed with the facility the first few times we went to visit her.

Within a few months, Nana had spent all of her savings and was now officially a Medicaid (welfare) patient. No longer on the first floor, Nana was "housed" on the second floor—away from the beautiful lobby with fresh flowers, the library with original works of art, and the community room. Our first impressions of a caring facility were suddenly replaced by genuine concern for her care as we noticed a "distinct odor" permeating the hallway. Not long after that, Nana became bedridden and within a few weeks of going on Medicaid, passed away.

Would Nana have deteriorated so fast if she had remained a private pay patient? We'll never know the answer to that question.

— *Eileen Hamm*

KEY POINTS

Who Pays for Long-Term Care?

➤ There are four sources for providing or paying for long-term care: family, welfare, personal assets, and long-term care insurance.

➤ Welfare coverage is only available after a person's assets have been depleted.

➤ Waiting lists for "Medicaid Only" beds are a reality because few states have enacted laws that prohibit admission policies based on source of payment.

➤ When considering Medicaid Planning, seek the services of a licensed attorney who utilizes the *Comprehensive Planning Approach* to long-term care.

➤ Heirs are often surprised to learn that they are required to reimburse a portion of their inheritance to repay the government for long-term care provided to their loved ones through the Medicaid program. This process is called "Estate Recovery."

➤ Long-term care insurance is specifically designed to cover long-term care expenses in adult day centers, at home, in an assisted living community, or in a nursing home.

➤ Medicare does not pay for long-term care. The program was established to pay for physician and hospital care and does not cover costs associated with care beyond 100 days.

➤ Medicare Supplement policies only cover services approved by Medicare and do not cover long-term care.

➤ Private health insurance specifically excludes coverage for long-term care. The maximum amount of benefit for care provided by health insurance is 100 days.

Chapter 5

Why Is Long-Term Care a Woman's Issue?
by Eileen Hamm

As a woman and a registered nurse, I know that the person who provides the care is generally the female. "We" usually means "she," especially when it comes to taking care of a spouse, parents of a spouse, or one's own parents.

— Eileen Hamm

Having a written long-term care plan is important for every family in America, but particularly for women. Almost always, the female takes ultimate responsibility for the day-to-day care of a family member who is ill or disabled. This is not sexist. This is not whining. It's a fact. In our years of working with financial professionals to assist families with LTC Planning, I have personally listened to the stories of women whose lives have been totally altered due to the long-term care needs of a loved one. Similar stories involving men are also becoming more common. But the majority of informal caregivers in our country—almost 72% of the estimated 7 million providers of care—are female.

When I talk with couples about planning for long-term care, they often exchange glances and say, "Oh, we'll take care of one another when the time comes." That pledge of mutual aid between spouses is touching, and without a doubt, sincere. But it normally comes from people who have yet to observe someone in their circle of family and friends move from independence to a need for care. Those who have observed others struggling with a long-term care need are typically driven to develop a definite plan for long-term care—and that plan rarely includes the option of relying on family.

My paternal grandmother, Nana, is a good example of how long-term care affects women. After my grandfather passed away, my father made sure Nana was safe and that she received the attention she needed. During the many years she was healthy, he took the place of his father by being "on call" to help with day-to-day living. He joined her during doctor visits, took her shopping, and called her every day. But when Nana's health declined and she needed assistance with personal care, my father's involvement lessened and my mother took over the major responsibilities of Nana's care. It was my mother, Nana's daughter-in-law, who handled the intimate tasks of helping her in and out of bed, bathing, and dressing her. This is a very typical pattern. As the level of required care grows more personal and intimate, the male caregivers in the family begin to feel uncomfortable, and the women take over the primary role of caregiver. Women tend to be more comfortable and skilled in this role, especially if they've also had children. But providing care comes at a heavy price: with the accompanying emotional and physical stress of being a caregiver, a women has a 63% higher risk of dying earlier than a woman of the same age who does not become a caregiver.

Women often sacrifice their social network and sense of well being to care for a loved one. It seems that every time I talk with my mother, who is now in her late 70s, she tells me about a sister or a friend "having an awful time" taking care of a spouse. These women tell her about the pure physical exhaustion they experience from caring for an adult on a daily basis. They suffer from the depression that comes from shouldering the responsibility alone, and they feel guilty for not being able to "do more."

But the prospect of becoming a caregiver should not be the only reason for women to ask their financial professional about LTC Planning for their family—it's also vital that they plan for *their own* care. Women make up the largest percentage of residents in all types of long-term care facilities, with the majority being widowed or divorced. Because we usually marry men at least a few years older than ourselves, and we live about seven years longer than men, by age 85, only 13% of women are still married.

By contrast, men make up the majority of people being taken care of at home. Normally, a wife or daughter helps her husband and parents through to the end. But her resources are limited when *she* needs long-term care. Unable to rely on informal, unpaid care from relatives at home, older women are usually forced to rely on more formal and costly solutions, such as a nursing home.

For example, although both my grandfathers lived to a ripe old age, neither of them spent time in a nursing home or other type of care facility. As both grandfathers became weaker and more debilitated due to old age and illness, my grandmothers once again found themselves in a mothering role, this time responsible for their husbands' daily care at home. By contrast, both my grandmothers spent their last years in care facilities, progressing from senior apartments to assisted living communities, and finally to a nursing home. This is the typical trend: a husband can generally count on receiving good care in his own home, provided by his spouse. If his wife can't provide the care personally, she will use their assets to hire and supervise full- or part-time caregivers.

Could I be a caregiver for my husband? Sure I could. Do I want to? No. Does this mean I care less for my spouse? That I'm a selfish person? No. It means I care enough to plan. To make sure my family and I have choices if someone we love requires long-term care.

Choices for women were limited in earlier generations. Thankfully, we now have access to the knowledge and resources needed to actively participate in planning ahead for our family's well being. We will always be "caretakers," but our role today includes careful advanced planning for the potential long-term care of our loved ones *and ourselves*. If we don't proactively plan ahead, the comfortable and healthy retirement we envision may be greatly altered, and even cut short by the consequences of providing or receiving long-term care.

KEY POINTS

Why Is Long-Term Care a Woman's Issue?

➤ The majority of informal caregivers in our country—almost 72% of the estimated 7 million providers of care—are female.

➤ Women make up the largest percentage of residents in all types of long-term care facilities.

➤ Men make up the largest percentage of people receiving care at home because a spouse, daughter, or daughter-in-law normally provides care for as long as possible.

➤ A female caregiver has a 63% higher risk of dying earlier than a woman of the same age who does not become a caregiver.

PART 2

The Only Effective Way to Plan for Long-Term Care

Let our advance worrying become advance thinking and planning.

— Winston Churchill

PART 2:
The Only Effective Way to
Plan for Long-Term Care

The LTC Planning industry is heavily influenced by the insurance industry because the foundation of today's LTC Planning is detrimentally rooted in the creation of LTC insurance. LTC insurance was invented and extensively promoted prior to the mass aging of America's population, which is ushering in the need to plan ahead.

This fact is responsible for millions of American families failing to have a plan for long-term care. To the detriment of American families, traditional insurance agents often promote such myths as "LTC insurance is for everyone." These agents normally use a *"single sales approach"* to long-term care, ignoring a family's overall personal and financial objectives.

The most effective way to plan for long-term care is to clearly view LTC Planning as an integral component of the financial and estate planning process. Embracing this viewpoint makes it apparent that the first person to initiate your plan for long-term care is your financial professional. Your advisor, who may be your Certified Financial Planner (CFP®), Certified Public Accountant (CPA), or Estate Planning Attorney, is familiar with your unique situation and can work with an LTC Planning expert to assure that your plan is integrated with your personal and financial objectives. This approach is called the **Comprehensive Planning Approach** to long-term care and is explained in *Chapter 7.*

Work with your financial professional and the LTC Planning expert they use as their resource to consider and evaluate your current financial situation, goals for the future, personal tolerance for risk, and health history. Once this analysis is complete, your most appropriate long-term care plan can be developed.

Chapter 6 Integrating Long-Term Care Planning with Financial and Estate Planning

With money and financial planning, prudence comes first.
— Benjamin Franklin

Financial planners, estate planning attorneys, and CPAs offer advice on a variety of financial topics. Your financial professional is the first person to initially assist you with learning about LTC Planning.

The following overview will explain why a written LTC Plan must become an essential component of every financial and estate plan.

A BRIEF OVERVIEW OF FINANCIAL AND ESTATE PLANNING

The financial and estate planning processes generally address three areas:

1. Saving and investing for retirement
2. Preserving and spending what is accumulated
3. Leaving an estate to heirs and beneficiaries

If money were no object, we would no doubt satisfy all of our desires. But for most of us, fulfilling all of our wants and goals would exceed our available resources. To achieve the best results, careful planning about how we allocate our money is required. In financial and estate planning, we integrate daily decisions about money with lifetime personal and financial goals and create a plan for achieving those goals.

Financial and estate planning is an overall process of setting goals, evaluating where we are with respect to those goals, laying out a plan to achieve them, implementing the plan, and modifying the plans and actions as our situation and goals change.

Financial planners, estate planning attorneys, and CPAs assist you in reaching your financial goals by advising you in one or more of the following 7 areas:

1. **Setting financial and estate planning objectives:** Evaluates your complete financial and estate planning picture. An analysis would consider budgeting, emergency fund planning, credit and debt management, education funding, and insurance planning. It would also analyze estate management, if your objective is to leave your estate to heirs or charity.

2. **Insurance planning and risk management:** Addresses three general areas of risk to the overall success of your financial and estate plan: risk to your family and other people you know; risk to your property; and risk to people you don't know and their property. Your financial advisor may explain that LTC Planning is a part of the Insurance planning and risk management component of your financial and estate plan.

FAST FACTS:

- Men and women who plan for the future—at all ages from 25 to 75 and with household incomes from $25,000 to $500,000—report increased personal life satisfaction.

- The National Council on Aging reports that a major worry of Americans over age 75 is that they will be required to spend all of their money on long-term care.

- **66%** of people who created an estate plan feel comfortable with their retirement security; only **37%** of those without an estate plan feel at ease.

3. **Employee benefits planning:** Analyzes the advantages and disadvantages of various types of employee benefit plans. This may include evaluating disability and medical insurance plans, and evaluating group or sponsored LTC insurance programs offered through your company or other "group."

4. **Investment planning:** Sets objectives, evaluates investment risk, investment strategies and vehicles such as mutual funds, stocks and bonds.

5. **Income tax planning:** Analyzes the tax consequences of investment planning, insurance planning, retirement and employee benefit planning, and estate planning.

6. **Retirement planning:** Integrates all aspects of financial and estate planning into a customized plan for financial independence.

7. **Estate planning:** Addresses tax-efficient ways to acquire, preserve, and transfer wealth to other parties, both during and after life. Estate planning can also address planning for incapacity due to a disability or the need for long-term care.

As you can see, LTC Planning could overlap several areas of your financial and estate plan.

SELECTING A FINANCIAL PROFESSIONAL

When selecting a financial professional, the most important considerations to understand are:

- The services provided: Many financial professionals create a comprehensive financial plan based on an analysis of your situation in regard to the 7 areas explained above. Generally, the financial professional specializes in one or two of the 7 areas and will assist you in implementing strategies in those specialty areas. For the remaining areas, they will refer you to the appropriate specialist(s).

- How the financial professional is compensated: Compensation to financial professionals can be based on an hourly rate, a management fee, a commission earned, or by some combination of these 3 models. The model that's most appropriate for you will depend on your unique circumstances.

It's generally recommended that you avoid financial professionals who try to do it all: sell insurance and financial products, manage your assets, and recommend estate planning strategies. Such financial professionals many times attempt to personally handle too many areas of financial and/or estate planning, which can result in poor to mediocre service in all areas. You are normally better served by a financial professional who specializes in narrow areas of expertise.

Most financial professionals limit their role in LTC Planning to informing and initially educating you about the need to have a plan for long-term care. Some financial professionals may also assist with evaluating and narrowing down the options that would be the most appropriate for you to consider. Then they refer you to an LTC Planning and Insurance expert certified in the *Comprehensive Planning Approach* to long-term care, who will assist you in the development and implementation of your LTC Plan. This expert should always provide a copy of the written plan to the financial professional and to appropriate family members.

For a complete checklist of questions to ask when selecting a financial professional, email us at: **fpchecklist@superiorltc.com**.

WHAT IF YOU DO NOT HAVE A FINANCIAL PROFESSIONAL?

The *Comprehensive Planning Approach* advises that you ask your financial planner, estate planning attorney, and/or CPA to provide you with initial guidance regarding LTC Planning. This recommendation presumes that you already have a relationship with one or more of these professionals. If you have not established such a relationship, ask your friends, family members, and associates for information about the financial professionals they use. If you are unable to locate a professional, contact us through our website and we will guide you to a local financial professional. Our website address is: **www.superiorltc.com**.

If the financial professional you use or the one you are referred to by someone else is not familiar with LTC Planning, inform them that we offer training and certification in the *Comprehensive Planning Approach* to qualified financial professionals. This training and certification teaches financial professionals how to educate and assist their clients with understanding their most suitable LTC Planning options.

KEY POINTS

Integrating Long-Term Care Planning with Financial and Estate Planning

➤ A written plan for long-term care must become an essential component of every financial and estate plan.

➤ A long-term care plan should always be developed within the context of your family's personal and financial objectives.

➤ The financial and estate planning process includes budgeting and saving for retirement, preserving assets during retirement, and leaving an estate to heirs, beneficiaries and/or charity.

➤ Your financial professional may explain that the insurance planning and risk management area of financial and estate planning is the primary area where planning ahead for long-term care fits into the overall financial and estate planning picture. But planning ahead for long-term care can also overlap several other areas of your financial and estate plan.

➤ Financial professionals normally limit their role in LTC Planning to informing and initially educating you about the need to have a plan for long-term care. Some may also assist you in narrowing down your options, prior to referring you to an LTC Planning and Insurance expert certified in the *Comprehensive Planning Approach* to long-term care.

Chapter  Planning Ahead Using the *Comprehensive Planning Approach*

You got to be careful if you don't know where you're going, because you might not get there.
— Yogi Berra

Who will provide your long-term care? Where will your care take place? Who will pay the bills? The long-term care industry is working to answer these questions and find solutions to the long-term care financing and delivery challenges of the next several decades. Unfortunately, solutions are not being developed in unison. The result is fragmentation, which has led to overall confusion and apathy about how to develop an effective written plan for long-term care.

Part of the solution to this problem is to develop your LTC Plan within the context of your personal and financial objectives. The ***Comprehensive Planning Approach*** was specifically designed to integrate LTC Planning with financial and estate planning. This approach has a proven track record for assisting you with the development of the most appropriate LTC Plan for you, based on a logical and emotional analysis of your unique situation. The alternative to planning ahead with this approach is to be manipulated by a *single sales approach* used by many insurance agents. Even worse is to have no plan at all, defaulting to options that completely expose your family to financial and emotional risks.

The most effective way to benefit from the *Comprehensive Planning Approach* is to first ask your financial professional for guidance. Your financial professional will likely answer some basic questions about LTC Planning and may initially assess the options that would be the most appropriate for you to consider. Then they will refer you to an LTC Planning expert.

The expert you are referred to should be specifically certified in the *Comprehensive Planning Approach* to long-term care. This certification program has been developed over a period of several years, with the guidance and advice of financial planners, CPAs, estate planning attorneys, and other experts, such as the professionals interviewed in *Chapter 19.*

Becoming certified to utilize this approach effectively requires many hours of study followed by examinations. But the overview of the 7 steps to the *Comprehensive Planning Approach* explained below will give you a solid foundation for understanding the most effective approach to planning ahead for long-term care.

SEVEN STEPS OF THE *COMPREHENSIVE PLANNING APPROACH*

1. Learn about Long-Term Care

Become knowledgeable about the issue of long-term care—what it is, where care can be received, and how much it costs in your area. *These subjects are discussed in Chapters 1 through 3.*

2. Evaluate the Implications of Relying on each of the 4 Resources

This is the heart of a truly effective plan for long-term care. Evaluate long-term care from the standpoint of your personal situation. How will the need for long-term care impact your family and your personal and financial objectives? Which of the four resources available to you for paying for a potential long-term care need appear to be appropriate for your situation? *(Family, welfare, personal assets, or LTC insurance. These subjects are discussed in Chapter 4.)*

3. Determine Your Preferred Payment and Care Options

As you evaluate the long-term care resources available to you, analyze and consider each one by asking, "If I had a need for long-term care tomorrow, where would the money come from to pay for my care, and who would provide my care?" For example, do you have family members who could provide your care? If so, decide who specifically will provide the care. Will you move in with one or more of your children? Or will they move in with you?

If you are considering using LTC insurance as your option, ask your financial professional to refer you to an LTC Planning and Insurance expert to evaluate whether or not you qualify for coverage and to assist you with the 6 steps outlined in *Chapter 11.*

4. Choose the Best Option and Develop Your Written Plan

The most appropriate option for your situation will become apparent after becoming knowledgeable about the issue, thoroughly understanding and analyzing your resources, and seriously pondering the fact that any one of us could suddenly have a need for long-term care at any time.

Using this thorough analysis, you will then make a choice as to how you will pay for care, and document the plan in writing.

5. Implement Your Plan

If your written plan calls for relying on welfare, set up an appointment with an attorney familiar with the process of Medicaid Planning and the new D.R.A. Legislation *(see Chapter 4: Who Pays For Long-Term Care?)*. If the plan calls for using your own assets, make sure your financial professional and family have a copy of your plan so that they know certain monies are earmarked and reserved to pay for your long-term care needs. If your plan calls for using LTC insurance, ask the LTC Planning and Insurance expert referred by your financial professional to help you design a customized LTC insurance policy *(see Chapter 11: Designing the Right Coverage)*.

6. Finalize Your Plan

If using welfare is your plan, finalize the details with your attorney. If LTC insurance is your plan, finalize your coverage. Regardless of the plan you develop, make sure each member of your family receives a copy of the plan. It's emotionally important for them to know in advance that you haven't left this important area of financial and estate planning to chance. Be specific with them and include the location of any policies, account numbers, funds earmarked for care, and the name, address, and phone numbers of your financial advisor(s) and/or LTC Planning and Insurance expert. It will most likely be your family members who will handle the details of implementing your plan at the time your care is needed. Providing them with all of this information is vital.

7. *Review Your Plan Annually*

Your plan must accomplish the objectives it was designed to achieve—today and in the future. Long-term care is not a static issue, and any plan put in writing today must be periodically reviewed. The *Comprehensive Planning Approach* includes a review of your plan at least annually, to ensure that it remains the appropriate solution in the years ahead.

A Family Affair

My wife Gail and I have both faced the emotionally challenging task of placing three parents in a facility. We learned firsthand that the need for care can happen to anyone, at anytime, and without warning.

One evening, we received a call from my sister informing us that my mother was in the hospital after having a stroke. Mother was 84, in relatively good health, but lived alone. After the stroke, she was not able to continue living by herself and we had to place her in a nursing home.

My wife's parents also needed long-term care. Parkinson's disease incapacitated my father-in-law and a hip replacement that did not heal as expected left my mother-in-law disabled. He didn't know it at the time, but my father-in-law inspired me to choose long-term care planning as a career. When my wife and I moved my in-laws from the home they had lived in for 40 years, my father-in-law said to me, "I sure wish we had planned for this." He was worried that all their hard-earned savings, accumulated over a lifetime, would be used to pay for care. Both parents died in the facility, having used all but $2,000 of their estate.

These experiences revealed to me that a need for long-term care is emotionally and financially devastating and that long-term care is really a "family affair". Having personally traveled this journey with my own family, I realize there is no substitute for planning in advance for long-term care.

— *Don Olson*

	The Comprehensive Planning Approach	A Single Sales Approach
Objective	• Determine most appropriate LTC Planning solution; document the plan in writing; review the plan annually	• Sell long-term care insurance
Considerations	• Overall personal and financial objectives • Insurance priorities • Risk tolerance philosophy • Cost of care in local area • Your health • Affordability analysis	• Your health • Affordability of insurance • Whether or not you can be easily influenced to buy long-term care insurance
Approach	• Solutions-based planning • Consultative; Educational • Emphasis placed on analyzing and documenting the best overall solution for your unique situation	• Pressure to purchase insurance • "Transaction" driven, with emphasis on having you make a "quick" decision
Financial Professional	• A CFP® (Certified Financial Planner), estate planning attorney, and/or CPA	• Usually not involved
Agent	• Recommended by your financial professional • Offers no other financial products or advice other than LTC Planning and LTC insurance • Specifically certified in the *Comprehensive Planning Approach* to long-term care • If LTC insurance is a consideration, independently licensed with several top-rated **only** companies	• A generalist insurance agent who may have contacted you by mail, cold call, or with some other marketing "scheme" • Normally sells LTC insurance plus other types of insurance and financial products • Education and training may be as minimal as basic requirements needed to sell LTC insurance • May represent only one company; or may represent several companies, regardless of the companies' financial ratings
Service	• Reviews plan annually for suitability and makes adjustments accordingly • Helps with claim's process if LTC insurance is part of your plan	• Rare contact with agent following the sale • Little to no assistance at time of claim

* This information is for general purposes only. You may meet agents or financial professionals who use a single sales approach, but still offer some of the characteristics and services used in the "Comprehensive Planning Approach."

KEY POINTS

Planning Ahead Using the *Comprehensive Planning Approach*

➤ Using the seven steps of the *Comprehensive Planning Approach* results in a written plan for long-term care that is integrated with your family's personal and financial objectives.

➤ The *single sales approach* may result in the purchase of LTC insurance when coverage is inappropriate; or the issuance of LTC insurance with inappropriate benefits.

➤ Seek the services of a financial professional who utilizes the *Comprehensive Planning Approach* to long-term care. They will likely refer you to an LTC Planning and Insurance expert, who will assist you in the development and distribution of your written plan for long-term care.

PART 3

Using Long-Term Care Insurance As Your Plan

In just two days,
tomorrow will be yesterday.

— Anonymous

PART 3:
Using Long-Term Care Insurance As Your Plan

INTRODUCTION: HISTORY OF THE LONG-TERM CARE INSURANCE INDUSTRY

The concept of insurance goes back to 3,000 BC when Babylonian merchants began pooling their funds to reduce the economic risks of losing caravans to pirates and thieves.

This ancient idea of *pooling* the financial resources of a group to reduce the economic *risks* faced by individuals created the foundation for today's insurance industry. Of course, the industry has evolved to a point of sophistication based on well-documented statistics and probabilities.

The LTC insurance industry is in its infancy compared to most types of insurance coverage. The foundation for today's LTC insurance began in 1965, and correlates directly with the enactment of Medicare. Medicare was established to deliver health insurance for those 65 and older and for certain people with disabilities.

The two major parts of Medicare are:

- **Part A:** coverage for Hospital and Skilled Nursing Home Care
- **Part B:** coverage for Physician's Services

Shortly after Medicare was enacted, the insurance industry discovered a marketing opportunity in the Part A Skilled Nursing Home Care benefit. The nursing home benefit offered by Medicare only pays for the first 20 days of skilled nursing home care. "Skilled Nursing Home Insurance" was invented to pay for skilled nursing home care needed beyond Medicare's 20 days of coverage.

As the name implies, the policies required that a person receive "skilled care" in order to collect policy benefits. Skilled care is only needed for the most serious types of health conditions.

The policies also required that:

- A person first spend at least three days in a hospital, prior to the nursing home confinement
- A person need skilled nursing home care beyond 20 days

Because a very small percentage of people who need skilled care actually stay in a nursing home for longer than 20 days, these policies rarely paid benefits. "Skilled Nursing Home Insurance" was deemed worthless by reputable financial professionals.

LTC INSURANCE EVOLVES TO VIABLE SOLUTION

During the 1980s, our federal and state legislators became justifiably concerned about health care financing for our aging population. As data from research on the issue of long-term care surfaced, it became increasingly apparent to legislators that Medicare's so-called long-term care benefit was designed to cover only short-term care. The looming long-term care threat—the potential of needing care for years, not weeks—encouraged legislators to focus on supporting the development of worthwhile LTC insurance.

By the late 1980s, laws were being passed that required LTC insurance policies to pay benefits irrespective of Medicare benefits. Further legislation required that policies cover all levels of care, not just skilled care. Long-term care insurance finally evolved to a real and viable solution for financing long-term care.

AWARENESS GROWS

Despite legislation leading to quality coverage, LTC insurance remained an obscure type of coverage. For the most part, the only people familiar with the term *long-term care* were those in need of it.

This lack of awareness abruptly changed in 1991. "Long-term care" became a well-known term during Bill Clinton's run for President. Clinton began his election campaign on a platform of health care reform. In speeches prior to his election, as well as during his first two years in office, he informed Americans about the lack of coverage for long-term care. In a typical speech, he would emphasize that, "Our proposed health care reform package will cover you for long-term care." By 1993, we had learned more about long-term care than most of us wanted to know.

We all know the rest of the story: by trying to solve America's entire health care crisis in one single package, Clinton and Congress were unable to resolve the major problems affecting health care.

But there was one unintentional positive outcome to the proposals: we learned that long-term care is expensive; and that the government is not prepared to foot the bill. These discoveries brought an intense interest in LTC insurance as a means of paying for long-term care. An industry that had previously received little public interest suddenly found itself in the limelight, with increasing demand for its once obscure coverage.

Up until this point, only about 20 insurance companies offered LTC insurance. As a result of the new interest and demand for coverage, over one hundred insurance companies entered the market. Soon, the competition between insurance carriers was fierce.

These new companies made some hasty decisions that benefited the consumer—at least temporarily. They reduced the overall average premium rate. And, eager to gain their share of the LTC insurance market, some insurance companies loosened their health-disqualifying restrictions, and began offering coverage to those with major health problems. For the first time, LTC insurance became available to those who were likely to need long-term care sooner rather than later.

GROWING PAINS FROM INEXPERIENCE

But like so many "booms," the frenzy was destined to "bust." These inexperienced insurance companies, once eager to serve an untapped market, began to feel the pains of improper pricing and underwriting. Substantial losses were incurred due to the claims of policyholders who were in poor health when the coverage was issued, and even poorer health a few years later. Although they continue to pay claims, and by law are required to honor all policies issued, most of these inexperienced companies exited the LTC insurance market as fast as they entered it.

When an insurance company decides to exit a market, it becomes a major cause for concern for their policyholders. The most serious concern is that premium rates will be raised to levels where the coverage is no longer affordable, due to adverse claims experience *(Adverse Selection is explained in Chapter 17: Group and Sponsored Long-Term Care Insurance)*.

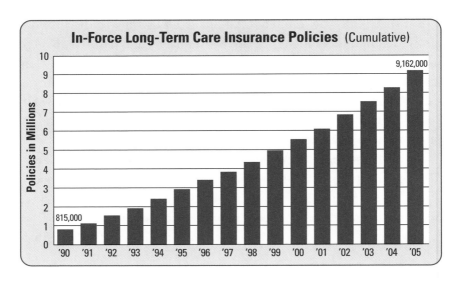

In-Force Long-Term Care Insurance Policies (Cumulative)

INDUSTRY MATURES

Although the number of LTC insurance companies remaining in the market today is small, these companies are much more committed to the industry. By following the guidelines for choosing a company explained in *Chapter 12*, consumers are in a good position to obtain coverage from an insurance company that has a reasonable underwriting and pricing philosophy. This will result in more stabilized premium rates.

Long-term care insurance protects almost 10 million individuals today. The combined coverage protects over $600 billion in assets. Cumulative benefits paid are over $15 billion, with over $1 billion paid in benefits in the year 2006 alone. These numbers will rise dramatically over the coming years, as more Americans choose LTC insurance as their option for paying for long-term care.

Our Promise

It was a promise all five children made to our mother— that we would never put her in a nursing home. All four of her sisters had lived into their late 90's and early 100's, so the chances were high that keeping our promise could have us caring for Mom for longer than any of us could imagine. My brother, who's a doctor, had the foresight to suggest that we look into options for paying for her care, "just in case" she ever needed it. After evaluating the four resources for paying for long-term care, we all decided that LTC insurance would be the best solution. All 5 children shared in the cost of the premium.

Mom was diagnosed with early Alzheimer's at 85 years old. Our normally fit and healthy mother was now frail and confused. Three of us are now taking turns having her live with us for 3-4 months at a time. If we hadn't planned ahead for her care, we would never be able to afford the supplemental assistance needed to care for her. With the option we chose, Mom is able to receive care in an adult day care center for up to 8 hours a day, 5 days a week. On weekends, we are able to hire aides to provide the respite we need from being "on duty" the full 24 hours a day.

As her disease progresses, we know that the emotional and physical demands on us and our families will be tremendous. But by planning ahead, we feel that we will have the resources we need to keep our promise.

— Michelle LaMarche

Chapter  Why People Choose Long-Term Care Insurance as Their Plan

Life is pleasant. Death is peaceful.
It's the transition that's troublesome.

— Isaac Asimov

The purpose of long-term care insurance is to protect and preserve a family's overall financial, emotional, and physical well-being. Insurance pays caregivers to assist with physically and emotionally exhausting tasks, reserving the family member's energy for providing a higher quality of emotional support to a loved one.

In the years since long-term care insurance has gained widespread acceptance, several surveys have been conducted to determine the *specific* reasons why people choose insurance as their plan for long-term care.

EFFECTS OF LONG-TERM CARE BASED ON GENDER

Virtually every survey reveals that women are initially much more receptive than men to plan ahead for long-term care. *Chapter 5* explained that long-term care is essentially a women's issue. Almost 72% of caregivers are women. Their average age is 48. The most likely recipient is her mother-in-law, and/or her own mother.

Women are more affected by the need for long-term care because:

- Women outlive men by an average of 7 years.
- The stress of caring for a loved one, normally her older spouse, strains a woman's health and many times directly or indirectly causes her to need long-term care.

Although caregiving provided by men is on the rise, men do not generally feel comfortable when they attempt to provide the physical and emotional care needed by a family member in need of care. So while women think ahead to the potential day-to-day physical and emotional aspects of care, men concentrate on the more logical aspects, including the financial consequences.

FAST FACTS:

- **50%** of adult children would be willing to use the money they have set aside for their own children's education to pay for a parent's long-term care expenses.

- The number of American households providing unpaid care has more than **tripled** over the past decade. Almost **72%** of these caregivers are women. The most likely recipient of care is the mother-in-law.

- The need for women to take time off work to care for aging parents has increased by **300%** over the past decade.

- **86%** of long-term care insurance policyholders know someone who has been a caregiver.

- **77%** of adults have saved for their retirement, while only **10%** have planned ahead for the greatest risk to their retirement security—long-term care.

Planning ahead can relieve our family of the physical, emotional, and the logical (financial) aspects of a potential need for care. Once the true impact of a long-term care event is understood, both men and women normally become motivated to create a plan for long-term care. This may lead to an analysis of the suitability for long-term care insurance *(see Chapter 9).*

THE MAJOR BENEFICIARIES OF PLANNING AHEAD

Our family is the major beneficiary of planning ahead because, in many cases, the person who needs care is not even aware of the need. They may be cognitively impaired or so frail that they don't understand the impact that their need for care is placing on their family.

The themes of "family" and "legacy" consistently surface when people are asked why they chose LTC insurance as their plan.

BENEFITS OF OWNING LTC INSURANCE
Protect Assets

A need for long-term care is normally paid for with cash, most often from assets accumulated for retirement. Paying for long-term care with these funds compromises a safe and secure retirement. *Protecting assets* is one of the most common reasons for planning with LTC insurance.

During pre-retirement planning, many couples purchase coverage to assure their principle will not be invaded, so the income their assets provide them is protected. Planning with insurance can allow a retired couple to more freely enjoy retirement without being concerned that a long-term care need by one spouse will alter a well-planned and secure retirement for the other spouse.

Maintain Independence

People who have firsthand experience with the challenges surrounding long-term care are the strongest advocates of planning ahead with LTC insurance. They have felt the impact of the overwhelming responsibilities that caring for a loved one brings.

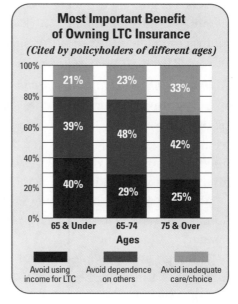

Most Important Benefit of Owning LTC Insurance
(Cited by policyholders of different ages)

The surveys reveal that many people purchase LTC insurance *after* caring for a loved one. The caregiving experience creates a strong desire to relieve family from the burdens of providing care.

"To maintain independence" gets to the heart of the true issue of LTC Planning. People who plan ahead are the same people who have carefully planned for other risks in their lives. They're guided by a need to ensure their independence and retain as much control as possible over their lives. The thought of having to rely on children or friends for lifestyle decisions and personal care is out of the question and acts as a strong motivator for securing a legacy of "independence."

Secure High-Quality and Affordable Care

As our society ages, the demand for high-quality care will sky-rocket. High-quality care may be more readily available to those who can guarantee payment with private funds—by using their own assets or by receiving benefits from an LTC insurance policy.

Long-term care insurance policyholders may have better access to high-quality providers who wish to maintain relationships with insurance companies because they provide them with steady work and guaranteed payment. Insurance companies offering LTC insurance are beginning to locate and contract with providers who have demonstrated high quality work and ethics. A provider screened and recommended by an LTC insurance company may provide better quality care than caregivers in the general population.

Maintain Current Living Arrangements

Long-term care insurance may also allow us to obtain the quality of care we need at home, without relying heavily on family and friends. Coverage may offer the peace-of-mind that many families need to ensure that quality care will be provided, without severely altering an existing lifestyle.

About 15% of LTC insurance purchasers cite *"maintaining current living arrangement for me and my family"* as the main reason for purchasing LTC insurance.

Although some people think of LTC insurance as "nursing home insurance," the major benefit of the coverage is having the ability to remain at home, or receive care in an assisted living community. This allows family members to maintain their current living arrangements, and minimize disruption, while still assisting with the emotional care of the loved one.

Maintaining the current living arrangements is also a major benefit to families who have children with physical or emotional disabilities. These families often plan with LTC insurance because their own need for long-term care could adversely affect the care of the disabled child.

CHILDREN AND PARENTS PLANNING FOR LONG-TERM CARE TOGETHER

The need for long-term care could not only deplete an inheritance, it may also affect the children's financial and career goals. To alleviate these problems, parents and children are beginning to feel comfortable discussing the issue of long-term care with one another.

But a survey conducted by the National Council on Aging revealed that there are distinct generational differences regarding the issue of how a parent's long-term care expenses would be funded. For example, 50% of adult children would be willing to use the money they have set aside for their own children's education to pay for a parent's long-term care expenses. This is clearly contrary to the desires of their parents. The survey revealed that 93% of parents would *not* want money set aside for their grandchildren's education to be used for their long-term care expenses. LTC insurance may offer security to both parents and children, by ensuring that education, retirement income, and inheritance dollars will not be invaded.

In some cases, children and parents are sharing in the cost of coverage. Estate planning attorney James Phillips *(see the interview in Chapter 19)* explains that the emotional issue

RELYING ON FAMILY FOR CARE

77% Would **not** want their children or spouse to care for them.

93% Would **not** want money saved for their grandchild's education to be used for their care.

86% Would **not** want children to tap their retirement savings to pay for their care.

91% Would **not** want children to sacrifice job advancement to pay for their care.

of inheritance, mixed with the stress of a potential need for long-term care, may provide the catalyst for grown children to consider paying for at least some of the LTC insurance premium for their parents. This may alleviate the potential problems that might arise among siblings once a parent requires long-term care.

Although inheritance and income protection are the rational reasons behind having "the long-term care conversation" with parents, the surveys pointed out that the primary motivation for grown children to consider sharing in the premium with their parents is the peace of mind of knowing their parents will have options for quality care. LTC insurance is purchased because the emotional and psychological benefits of knowing their parents will be cared for outweigh the cost of the premiums.

Second Marriages

Since the number of second marriages is growing at a faster pace than ever, the need for long-term care by one partner could cause problems among children of both spouses. The likelihood is high that the older partner will need long-term care services for several years because it's common for one partner in second marriages to be considerably younger than the other. Children born of the previous marriage(s) of the younger spouse may be apprehensive that their parent's health could be affected by providing care for an older spouse, or that an inheritance will be depleted paying for care for the older stepparent. Prenuptial agreements *will not* prevent the couple from having to *"spend down"* their combined assets before qualifying for welfare.

Planning ahead with LTC insurance for both partners of a second marriage can alleviate many of these concerns by assuring that neither spouse will be required to provide care personally or deplete their assets paying for the partner's care. This allows both partners to protect their mental and physical health, and to pass their assets down to their own bloodline.

Planning As A Family

The call couldn't have come at a worse time. With an infant and a newborn, both my husband and I were stretched beyond limits. So I immediately went into crisis mode when I heard my brother say, "Dad needs help at home. He keeps forgetting to take his heart medication."

As the "girl" in the family, I would normally be expected to assume the role of primary caregiver. But our current situation, with 2 babies and demanding careers, would make it very difficult for us to provide on-going care for Dad. Many families today are in the same situation as we are: spread across the globe, with children to care for, and 2 careers needed to support the family financially.

Fortunately, we had prepared ahead of time: Years earlier we had the "long-term care conversation" with my parents. We began by telling the story of a family we all knew who was dealing with a long-term care need. This offered us a natural opening for asking my parents if they had discussed the issue of long-term care with one another.

Our conversation was vague at first, but with the help of their financial planner, we developed a written plan for long-term care. It described their deliberate choices for how their care would be provided and paid for. We then communicated the plan to my siblings by providing each one with a written copy of the plan.

At the time, my brother who was now making the call, had made comments about the whole "LTC Plan thing" being "insensitive" and "depressing". He was now expressing his gratitude for having had the conversation years earlier.

— *Liz Turner*

> # KEY POINTS

Why People Choose Long-Term Care Insurance as Their Plan

➤ The real beneficiary of long-term care planning is not us; it's our family, and in most cases female family members.

➤ People who plan ahead with long-term care insurance want to protect their assets, maintain their independence, secure high-quality and affordable care, maintain their current living arrangements, and/or protect their children's income, assets, and inheritance.

➤ Children and parents many times plan ahead for long-term care together for the protection of the relationship they have with one another, as well as for financial reasons.

➤ Many partners of a second marriage choose long-term care insurance for the purpose of assuring that neither spouse will be required to personally provide care or deplete their assets paying for a partner's care. This allows both spouses to remain independent and pass assets down to their own bloodline.

Chapter 9: Is Long-Term Care Insurance Suitable for You?

Ninety percent of the game is half mental.
— Yogi Berra

In considering LTC insurance as an option to plan for long-term care, what is the best age to purchase insurance? Is there a net worth high enough to eliminate LTC insurance as an option for planning ahead for long-term care? These are the questions most commonly asked by people considering LTC insurance.

The answers people receive to these questions and many others regarding the suitability of insurance are varied and most of the time wrong. Beware of advisors who give black-and-white answers such as, "If you are younger than X, or older than Y, don't consider coverage," or, "If your assets are under X or greater than Y, don't consider LTC insurance."

There is a specific strategy for determining whether or not LTC insurance is suitable for you and your family. Your best defense against purchasing coverage you may not need, or going without coverage you should have, is to consult with your financial professional, not an insurance agent. Working with your financial professional and the LTC Planning and Insurance expert referred to you by your advisor ensures that the plan you develop will be the most appropriate plan for you. That plan may or may not include LTC insurance.

Insurance agents who sell LTC insurance using a *single sales approach* will debate the information in this section. They will tell you that you don't need to go through a "process" prior to considering LTC insurance. But the *Comprehensive Planning Approach,* developed over a period of 18 years with the assistance and advice of carefully selected financial planners, estate planning attorneys, and CPAs, has a proven track record as the best approach for determining your suitability for LTC insurance.

FAST FACTS:

- For every year you wait to purchase coverage, your effective premium will be **14%-22%** higher.

- The percentage of people healthy enough to pass underwriting is considerably less at age 70 than at age 60.

- One in three people between age 75 and 80 will not qualify for coverage because of health conditions.

- The New York State Partnership Program recommends that you allocate no more than **7%** of your annual income to long-term care insurance premiums.

The information in this chapter is to be used only as a preliminary guide before having a discussion with your financial professional and the LTC Planning and Insurance expert they recommend. This evaluation process does not replace the personal planning session you should have with these professionals to determine LTC insurance suitability for you.

PRIORITIZING YOUR INSURANCE NEEDS

The *Comprehensive Planning Approach* views LTC Planning as an integral part of the financial and estate planning process. Within the seven areas of financial and estate planning explained in *Chapter 6*, LTC insurance falls specifically into the area of "risk management." Risk management is the process of deciding how to control financial risk, and whether or not to transfer certain risks to an insurance company.

An evaluation of the suitability of LTC insurance will be inaccurate unless it first addresses the subject of "risk management prioritization." This is a process for prioritizing your insurance needs. At first, this discussion may seem out of place in a book about LTC Planning. But every family has a set of insurance needs that must be analyzed and prioritized before considering LTC insurance.

The following is our list of the most important types of personal insurance, in order of priority:

1. Health Insurance: Anything can happen to our health at any time. No one in our country should be without health insurance because unexpected illnesses or accidents carry a hefty price tag. Health insurance helps a financially comfortable family remain secure, by covering unexpected hospital and physician charges that could otherwise devastate their financial future. No other type of personal insurance is more important.

2. ***Disability Income Insurance:*** If you are working and earning an income, disability income insurance can replace a portion of your income if you become disabled and are unable to work. For people earning a working income, a risk management plan that replaces the income of the breadwinners is imperative. Disability income insurance is designed to protect a working income.

   What if you are not earning a working income? If you are retired, and/or are living on investment income, disability income insurance is not important. In fact, it's not even available. Disability income insurance replaces a *working income.* If you are not working for an income, this type of insurance is not applicable to you.

3. ***Life Insurance:*** If you are earning a working income and have children or others who are dependent upon your income, your death would mean financial hardship for these people. Life insurance is designed to relieve that hardship, and is potentially your third most important type of insurance. Your financial professional may have other reasons for advising you to purchase life insurance, such as to pay estate taxes. But if your reason for needing life insurance is other than to protect your dependents from hardship, life insurance protection should be moved to a lower priority on this insurance priority list.

4. ***Long-Term Care Insurance:*** LTC insurance falls to as low as number four on our list of insurance priorities. You should consider LTC insurance only after you and your financial professional have analyzed your need and suitability for the above three types of personal insurance protection.

If you have yet to prioritize and plan ahead for your most important types of insurance, we recommend that you address those potentially higher priority risk-management topics before continuing to learn about LTC Planning and insurance.

If you and your financial advisor have determined that your insurance and risk management priorities are in order, it's now appropriate to analyze your suitability for LTC insurance.

ANALYZING THE SUITABILITY OF LONG-TERM CARE INSURANCE

Our approach to LTC insurance suitability uses a process of elimination to analyze whether or not to consider coverage. We begin by considering whether or not you qualify for coverage based on your current health. If you do not qualify, it makes little difference whether or not you are otherwise suitable for insurance. Analyzing the other aspects of coverage would be a waste of your time.

We then consider whether or not you can afford the premium. If you can't afford the premium, again there is no reason to consider the other aspects of LTC insurance.

This process of elimination continues by analyzing other factors. As you review the information, you may decide that you are "disqualified" at some point. If you do, speak with your financial professional and the LTC Planning and Insurance expert they work with to confirm your conclusion and to discuss alternative LTC Planning options.

REASONABLY GOOD HEALTH IS REQUIRED

Long-term care insurance is a health-qualifying type of insurance. You must be in reasonably good health in order to obtain coverage. If your health is not good enough to qualify for coverage, no amount of premium you are willing to pay will change the fact that you're ineligible. As with all types of insurance, many times those who want coverage the most are those who can't qualify for it.

If you decide to apply for coverage, you will go through a process called underwriting. *Underwriting* is defined as "a process of examining, accepting, or rejecting insurance risks, and then classifying those accepted in order to charge the proper amount of premium."

The LTC insurance underwriting process consists of answering questions about your health, and may also include a physical exam and/or a request for medical information from your doctor. *(The entire underwriting process is explained in Chapter 13.)*

If you currently have certain health conditions, you will automatically be ineligible to apply for LTC insurance. The *Disqualifying*

Disqualifying Health Conditions

You will **not qualify** for long-term care insurance if **presently,** or during the **12-month period preceding** the application for coverage, you needed any of the following:

- Assistance with any Activities of Daily Living ("ADLs" include: eating, bathing, dressing, toileting, continence, and transferring)
- Home Health Care Services
- Care in a Nursing Home or Assisted Living Community
- A walker, wheelchair, medical appliance, kidney dialysis machine, or a manufactured source of oxygen
- Treatment for any of the following conditions:

  - AIDS
  - Alzheimer's Disease
  - Acute and unspecified renal failure
  - Acute cerebral vascular disease
  - Congestive heart failure
  - Cirrhosis of the liver
  - Chronic memory loss
  - Chronic renal failure
  - Diabetes Mellitus with complications
  - Mental retardation

  - Multiple strokes
  - Multiple Sclerosis, other bone disease, and musculoskeletal disease
  - Muscular Dystrophy
  - Paralysis
  - Parkinson's Disease
  - Schizophrenia and related disorders
  - Senility and organic mental disorders
  - Severe Emphysema
  - Transient Ischemic Attack

Health Conditions chart offers some of the most common types of conditions that will exclude a person from obtaining LTC insurance. This list is not all-inclusive. Even if you answer "no" to all of these conditions, it does not mean that you will automatically qualify for coverage. Underwriting for LTC insurance is performed on an individual basis, and there may be other conditions, or combinations of conditions, that cause an application to be declined.

The LTC insurance industry is experiencing a trend toward more stringent underwriting. As new health information is released, insurance companies gain more insight into the reasons people need long-term care. For example, a recent study found that people who have diabetes are at greater risk for developing memory loss. This study will likely prompt other such studies, to research the link between diabetes and cognitive performance.

Keep in mind that this discussion is limited strictly to your current health. If you develop a health condition(s) *after* your LTC insurance policy is issued, the company cannot cancel your policy or deny a claim due to the newly developed condition.

AGE IS A FACTOR IN UNDERWRITING

While everyone should have a written plan for long-term care, your current age may determine whether or not you plan ahead with LTC insurance. Passing health underwriting is heavily influenced by age. The older we become, the more likely we are to develop health conditions that will exclude us from obtaining coverage. For example, the chart below shows that the percentage of people who are healthy enough to pass underwriting is considerably less at age 70 than at age 60.

The data also show that women are less likely to qualify for LTC insurance in almost all age brackets. This is because women often become caregivers, and providing care has a negative effect on a person's health.

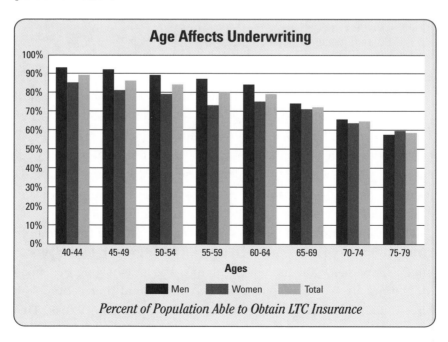

Percent of Population Able to Obtain LTC Insurance

AFFORDABILITY OF LONG-TERM CARE INSURANCE BASED ON AGE

Premium rates for LTC insurance have a reputation for being "high" and may be unaffordable to some people. This is usually due to the fact that people postpone investigating coverage until they are too old to receive a reasonable premium rate. The younger you are when you purchase LTC insurance, the lower your premium will be for the life of the policy. For every year you wait to purchase coverage, your

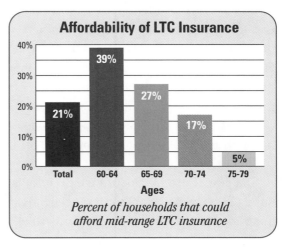

Affordability of LTC Insurance

Percent of households that could afford mid-range LTC insurance

premium will be 8-15% higher. But this percentage does not include the fact that there is an overall upward trend in premium rates in the industry as a whole. When you include this upward trend in premium rates, for every year a person waits to purchase coverage, they will pay an additional 14% to 22% in premium. This means that if a 55 year old who purchases coverage in 2007 would have purchased coverage in 2002, when they were age 50, their premium would be almost 50% less.

It can be a costly mistake to "wait until a certain age" to consider coverage. Some people heeding the advice to wait until the "perfect" age will develop health conditions that disqualify them from obtaining coverage and/or will reach an age where premiums are unaffordable.

Most people are surprised to learn that the total *cumulative* premium you will pay the insurance company over your lifetime is lower if you purchase coverage now compared to waiting until you're older. For example, if a 50-year-old purchases coverage today and pays premiums until life expectancy, they will pay less total *cumulative* premium to the insurance company than a 60-year-old who purchases coverage today and pays premiums until life expectancy. In addition, the 50-year-old is more likely to qualify for coverage and be offered preferred rates based on better health.

Many financial advisors will accurately point out that this example does not consider that the 60-year-old could save, invest, and earn interest on the premium amount over the 10-year period, instead of paying premiums. But it also does not consider that the 50-year-old could have a claim and collect benefits on the policy during the 10-year period. This "cumulative premium" example is purposefully simple, and is designed to point out that waiting until the "perfect age" to buy coverage can be a financial mistake. (For an in-depth explanation of the potential problems of waiting until the "perfect age," see *Chapter 18: LTC Planning and Insurance Myths.*)

Can you afford LTC insurance premiums at your age? As you evaluate LTC insurance, your financial advisor or LTC Planning and Insurance expert will provide you with a ballpark premium rate for coverage. Keep in mind that this initial figure will be an estimate only and should not be construed as the actual premium rate you will pay if you decide to purchase coverage. However, the ballpark rate will allow you to determine whether or not coverage is likely affordable for you.

Some people ask, "What percentage of my family's income should I allocate to LTC insurance premiums?" This will vary, depending on your situation. One guideline offered by the New York State Partnership *(see Chapter 16: Partnership Programs)* recommends that you allocate no more than 7% of your annual income to LTC insurance premiums. This guideline should be used for general purposes only. You and your financial advisor should work with an LTC Planning and Insurance expert to determine an appropriate income/premium allocation, based on your unique financial situation.

Are people in some age brackets better suited for choosing LTC insurance as their LTC Planning option than people in other age brackets? Yes, mainly due to insurance priorities and income. The fact that younger people tend to have insurance priorities that rank higher than LTC insurance makes younger people less likely to be able to afford LTC insurance, even though premium rates are fairly inexpensive.

The following is general information, based on our experience regarding age and suitability for coverage. The outcome of using the *Comprehensive Planning Approach* may determine that you fall into a different circumstance than the ones described.

Under age 45: People under age 45 rarely purchase LTC insurance because they fall into the category of having other higher-priority risks that must be covered by insurance. If they have properly prioritized their insurance needs, LTC insurance may be a type of insurance that they simply can't afford at this stage of their lives.

Another reason people in this age bracket rarely purchase coverage is that they are not aware of the risk. Few people in this age group have had a direct experience with long-term care so they are unaware of the need to plan ahead for their own care.

Some people in this age bracket do purchase coverage through a workplace, group, or sponsored offering. Unfortunately, because the *Comprehensive Planning Approach* is rarely utilized with these types of programs, there is no integration with the family's personal and financial objectives. If you are being offered coverage through your workplace, or any group or sponsored offering, read *Chapter 17: Group and Sponsored Long-Term Care Insurance* and speak with your financial advisor prior to purchasing the coverage.

Between age 45 and 65: This is the fastest-growing age bracket for planning ahead with LTC insurance. People between 45 and 65 have normally met the three most important criteria for choosing LTC insurance as their planning option:

1. All their other insurance risks have been prioritized and are adequately covered.
2. They are still young enough to be in good to excellent health and qualify for coverage.
3. They can afford the LTC insurance premium.

People in this age bracket are also more aware of the need to plan ahead because they experience the highest percentage of parents or other relatives and friends in need of long-term care. People who experience a long-term care event in their circle of family and friends are highly motivated to develop a plan for long-term care for themselves and their own families.

Between age 65 and 75: People in this age bracket should strongly consider the appropriateness of LTC insurance as soon as possible. The major hurdle facing these people is qualifying for coverage. As illustrated in the *Age Affects Underwriting Chart* (see previous section "Age is a Factor in Underwriting"), people who wait until later years to consider coverage take the risk of becoming uninsurable due to a health condition(s).

The second major hurdle for people in this age bracket is premium affordability. Premiums increase significantly at these older ages with every succeeding birthday. Coverage is likely to be unaffordable for people who investigate coverage in this age bracket.

Most people in the 65- to 75-year-old age bracket are in one of two situations:

1. They have already investigated LTC insurance and have either purchased coverage, or have made the decision to plan ahead with an alternative option.

2. They are suddenly highly motivated to investigate, or re-investigate coverage for a specific reason. For example, they or a loved one, or someone close to them has developed a health condition that has heightened their awareness of the need for long-term care. Hopefully, the person who is experiencing the health condition is not the same person who is seeking coverage. We receive inquiries on a daily basis from financial professionals with clients in this situation. Many times, the person inquiring about coverage investigated LTC insurance years earlier, but did not purchase coverage. Now, due to a decline in their health, they are motivated to buy coverage, but are uninsurable.

Over age 75: Most LTC insurance claims are submitted between age 79 and 85. For this reason, insurance companies are not anxious to issue coverage to people who have waited until age 75 or older to apply for LTC insurance.

One in three people between age 75 and 80 will not qualify for coverage due to existing health conditions. After age 80, odds are better than 50% that a person will not qualify for coverage. If they do qualify, chances are the premium will be much higher than they are willing or able to pay. If you are in this age group and want to consider LTC insurance, ask your financial advisor and LTC Planning and Insurance expert to analyze and offer some co-insurance options for making the premium more affordable.

YOUR "RISK TOLERANCE" PHILOSOPHY

Your risk tolerance philosophy is an important psychological consideration when determining whether or not to own LTC insurance. Some people have a high tolerance for financial risk, while others believe in a conservative approach and would prefer to transfer a risk to an insurance company.

People who have covered their other high-priority risks with insurance usually have a low tolerance for the financial risk of long-term care. Their philosophy is to maintain as much financial control as possible and to plan ahead for long-term care with insurance.

To understand your risk tolerance philosophy, ask your financial professional to assist you with analyzing and answering these questions:

- Have I consistently insured my family and myself for the proper types and amounts of insurance coverage such as health, disability, and life insurance?
- If I have, do I tend to transfer the entire risk to the insurance company, or am I comfortable insuring some of the risk myself? In other words, should I consider co-insuring the long-term care risk?

WHY DO WEALTHY PEOPLE CONSIDER LTC INSURANCE?

If you have enough money to pay for your own long-term care needs, should you consider LTC insurance as your plan for long-term care?

Many people are surprised to learn that there is **no upper limit** to the amount of assets you should own before you **automatically** choose to self-insure for long-term care. Thousands of wealthy people have purchased LTC insurance even though they have the financial ability to pay for care.

Wealthy people often purchase coverage for reasons that are much different than the rest of the population. But one of the major reasons many wealthy people purchase coverage is to plan in advance for some of the major decisions that must be made by the sudden need for long-term care. For example, the long-term care coordination benefit included with some LTC insurance policies can help simplify the process of finding quality care providers *(see Chapter 14: Submitting a Claim)*.

Many people, including some well-intentioned financial professionals, analyze LTC insurance from a strictly logical point of view, and place coverage strictly in the category of "insurance to protect assets." Although protecting assets is a common reason for purchasing coverage, some wealthy people also have a variety of psychological reasons for planning ahead with LTC insurance.

We have asked many high-net-worth individuals and families the following question about why they decided to purchase LTC insurance:

Q. "Since you have the assets necessary to pay for long-term care without buying insurance, why are you purchasing LTC insurance?

Here are some of their answers:

A1. "We have always been planners. We've taught our children to plan ahead. Even though we could pay for the cost of care ourselves, we want to leave a legacy that is consistent with our lifelong philosophy of planning for the future."

A2. "All my life, I've used other people's money to succeed. For example, while some of my colleagues avoided borrowing to leverage financial opportunities, I've succeeded by borrowing and then investing that money for our future. I view the purchase of LTC insurance with this same philosophy: long-term care is a high-probability risk, and if I can spend $3,000 per year in exchange for a potential $70,000 per year in benefits, I view that as leverage."

A3. "By purchasing coverage now, I lock in a lower premium rate for the rest of my life. Even though I could self-insure for all long-term care expenses today, that could change in the future. With insurance, if my investments decline in value, I won't have to worry about invading our principle to pay for long-term care expenses."

A4. "We were fortunate to learn about LTC insurance while we were young and after becoming caregivers for one of our parents. We were also able to write off the premium on our corporate tax return. When our CPA analyzed the bottom line numbers, it made good fiscal sense."

A5. "The 'Care Coordination Benefit' of the LTC insurance policy helps my family find quality caregivers if we have a claim. This benefit alone is worth the price of the policy."

The most appropriate LTC Planning option for you and your family is a personal issue. The option you choose has as much to do with your psychological characteristics as it does the amount of your assets. People who plan ahead and achieve a successful lifestyle are more likely to plan ahead for long-term care. For some, LTC insurance makes sense even if they have sufficient assets to pay for their own care.

For more insight into why wealthy people may consider LTC insurance, read *Chapter 18: LTC Planning and Insurance Myths.*

SEEK ADVICE FROM YOUR FINANCIAL PROFESSIONAL

The only effective way to develop a plan for long-term care is to ask for assistance from your financial professional and the LTC Planning and Insurance expert referred by your financial professional. These professionals can explain your various options for paying for long-term care, and assist you in evaluating your suitability for LTC insurance.

If an advisor automatically tells you "No, don't consider LTC insurance," without helping you analyze your unique situation, locate another financial advisor—one who utilizes the *Comprehensive Planning Approach* to long-term care.

If your advisor tells you "Yes, you should consider LTC insurance," ask them to refer you to an LTC Planning and Insurance expert who can assist you with a complete analysis.

KEY POINTS

Is Long-Term Care Insurance Suitable for You?

➤ Before considering long-term care insurance, confirm that your other risks have been prioritized, based on your family's unique circumstances.

➤ The most important types of personal insurance coverage, in order, are health insurance, disability income insurance, life insurance, and long-term care insurance.

➤ If you are in poor health, no amount of premium you are willing to pay will change the fact that you're ineligible for long-term care insurance.

➤ The total *cumulative* premium you will pay over your lifetime for long-term care insurance is lower if you purchase coverage now compared to waiting until you're older.

➤ Premiums significantly increase at older ages and with every succeeding birthday. Coverage is likely to be unaffordable for people who investigate insurance at older ages.

➤ Wealthy people often plan ahead with long-term care insurance for psychological reasons such as expanding their choice of quality care options.

Chapter 10 The Essentials of Long-Term Care Insurance

*Things which matter most must never be
at the mercy of things which matter least.*

— Goethe

A basic education about how LTC insurance works will provide you with a foundation for having a meaningful discussion with your financial planner, estate planning attorney, or CPA about developing your specific plan.

The essentials of LTC insurance are easier to understand when broken down into the factors that make up the coverage and impact the premium. There are seven basic factors to consider. Each factor has a direct bearing on how much you will pay for the coverage. Some of the factors will determine how much you will receive at the time of a claim.

There are also a number of optional benefits that can be considered with an LTC insurance policy. These "bells and whistles" are discussed at the end of the chapter.

SEVEN BASIC FACTORS INFLUENCING THE PREMIUM OF A LONG-TERM CARE INSURANCE POLICY:

1. How does the policy pay benefits?
2. Where can you receive care?
3. What is your current age?
4. How is your current health?
5. How much will the policy pay in benefits per day, week, or month?
6. How long will the policy pay benefits?
7. What is the policy elimination period?

FAST FACTS:

- The importance of proper plan design in a long-term care insurance policy will become evident, and sometimes painful, at claim's time.

- If not for the home care coverage provided by their long-term care insurance, **60%** of policyholders would not be able to afford to remain in their homes and would be forced to move to a care facility.

- Inflation is the most serious threat to a solid LTC Plan.

BALANCING THE FACTORS

The importance of balancing and prioritizing the seven factors can't be over-emphasized. Many people are in the unfortunate position of being both underinsured and overinsured, all in the same plan. This is because the agent selling the coverage did not properly balance and prioritize the factors and benefits at the time the policy was purchased. At claim's time the importance of properly balancing these factors and benefits will become evident, and sometimes painful. We illustrate this with a case study in *Chapter 11: Designing the Right Coverage.*

RATING THE IMPORTANCE OF THE FACTORS

Because some LTC insurance factors are much more important than others, we have devised a numerical icon to rate the importance of each of the factors. We call this assignment an "Importance Rating." A rating of 5 means that the factor is very important in the overall policy design process. A rating of 1 means that it is relatively insignificant.

This rating process is heavily influenced by our opinion and experience. Some people will point out instances where these recommendations would have been detrimental at the time of claim. In this regard, LTC insurance is like all other types of insurance: if you ever have a claim on a policy of any kind, you'll wish you had purchased the maximum benefits available in every category. But we give these recommendations without the foresight of knowing whether or not you will ever collect on your policy. Based on our 18 years of policy design and claim's experience, we believe the following recommendations offer a good balance between coverage choices and premium costs.

1. HOW DOES THE POLICY PAY BENEFITS?

Importance Rating:

Long-term care insurance policies have three basic methods of paying benefits:

1. With the **reimbursement method,** also known as the expense incurred method, you first pay the care provider, whether it be a facility or the person(s) caring for you at home. Then you submit a copy of the receipt to the LTC insurance company for reimbursement. Your reimbursed amount will be either the actual amount you paid for services or your in-force "benefit amount," whichever is less. "Benefit Amount" is explained in number 5, below.

2. With the **indemnity method,** no receipts are needed. The benefit paid to you is the exact amount of your in-force benefit amount, even if your long-term care expenses are less than your benefit amount.

3. With the **cash method,** you are not even required to incur expenses to receive benefits on a claim. You can collect your full benefit amount, even if someone cares for you free of charge.

These three methods of payment are listed in order of least to most expensive in premium cost. They are also listed in order from the least to greatest amount of potential money you could receive from an insurance claim. This is where the differences end. For example, when it comes to eligibility for collecting on the policies, all three methods are the same: It's neither easier nor harder to become eligible for benefits based on the payment method of the policy.

Recommendation

On the surface, indemnity and cash method policies appear to have an advantage, since they allow you to make a profit on a claim. But the reimbursement, or expense incurred method, is actually your best value because it does the most effective job of solving the true long-term care problem, per premium dollar paid.

Two specific reasons to avoid policies that pay on the indemnity and cash methods are:

1. Your initial premium will be higher—in most cases, significantly higher. This is because these policies make it possible for you to earn a profit on a claim by paying you a dollar amount higher than your actual costs, or in the case of cash method policies, paying you even if you do not incur expenses for care.

2. Not only will your initial premium be higher, indemnity and cash method policies will also be subject to more frequent and higher rate increases than policies that pay with the reimbursement method. This is because LTC insurance policies are placed in separate "pools," for claims experience. The method of payment, as well as other factors determines the policies' "pool." Indemnity and cash method policies will always be placed in a "pool" that is subject to paying higher and more frequent claims, making them susceptible to more frequent and higher rate increases.

2. WHERE CAN YOU RECEIVE CARE?

Importance Rating: **5**

The "type" of LTC insurance policy determines where you can receive long-term care services:

1. *"Home Care Only"* policies pay for care only in your home.

2. *"Facility Care Only"* policies pay for care only in a facility, such as an assisted living community or nursing home.

3. *"Comprehensive Long-Term Care Insurance"* policies pay for care in any setting, regardless of where the care is received (home, and/or assisted living communities and/or nursing homes).

If a need for long-term care arises, most people want to stay in their own home to receive care. In a national survey funded by the Office of Disability, Aging and Long-Term Care Policy, and the Robert Wood Johnson Foundation, it was learned that in the absence of home care benefits provided by their LTC insurance policy, 60% of individuals collecting on their policy could not afford to remain in their homes and would be forced to move to a facility *(LTCi Sales Strategies magazine, Vol. 3, No. 2, reprinted with permission, www.LTCSales.com)*. No one wants to be forced to move from their home to an assisted living community or a nursing home, simply because their policy lacked benefits for at-home care. For this reason, home care benefits are an essential component of an LTC insurance policy. But in many instances, home care is not an option, and a person must be moved to an assisted living community or a nursing home.

Recommendation

Since you do not know exactly where your care can be received, we recommend only the third option, the *"Comprehensive Long-Term Care Insurance"* policy. Only considering comprehensive long-term care insurance is **one of the most important recommendations in this book.** Comprehensive LTC insurance offers the best value because benefits will be paid to cover skilled and non-skilled providers in your home, assisted living communities, and nursing homes. These policies may also pay for care in community-based settings such as board-and-care homes and adult day centers.

Look for the words *"Comprehensive Long-Term Care Insurance Policy"* displayed prominently on the front of your policy and/or the forms and materials provided to you at the time you apply for coverage. If you see this terminology, you are considering the right type of policy because it will pay benefits in any setting. If you see any other term, such as "Home Care Only Insurance Policy," or "Nursing Home Only Insurance Policy," *do not* purchase the coverage unless your financial advisor and LTC Planning and Insurance expert have given you *specific* reasons for deviating from the recommendation to only consider "Comprehensive Long-Term Care Insurance."

3. WHAT IS YOUR CURRENT AGE?

Importance Rating:

Your **current age** will have a major impact on your LTC insurance premium. The younger you are when you purchase coverage, the lower your premium will be for the life of the policy.

When you purchase LTC insurance, you "lock-in" your issue-age premium rate for the rest of your life. This means that a 50-year-old who purchases coverage today will still be paying the 50-year-old premium rate, even when they are 75 years of age.

Important Clarification: Although you lock-in your current age rate when you purchase LTC insurance, premium rates *can* increase after the policy is issued. If an insurance company has underpriced their premiums or issued coverage to individuals with health problems, you will likely experience rate increases on your policy. But the rate increases will be on the entire "class" of policyholders. This means that everyone in your state who purchased a policy with your "policy form" from the same company will also receive a rate increase. The rate increase will always be a percentage of the amount of your current premium amount. This results in a "real dollar" rate increase that will be lower if you purchased coverage at a younger age.

When considering LTC insurance, ask your financial advisor and LTC Planning and Insurance expert about the recommended company's history of rate increases. Many insurance companies have an excellent record of premium stability, and you should consider **only** one of these top-rated companies *(for more on this subject, read Chapter 12: Choosing the Right Insurance Carrier).*

Recommendation

Although there are advantages to purchasing at a younger age, this does not mean that you should automatically purchase LTC insurance simply because you are young and can lock-in a low premium rate. LTC insurance suitability is thoroughly explained in *Chapter 9* and includes such considerations as prioritizing your insurance risks prior to considering coverage.

But if it is determined that LTC insurance is suitable for you, purchasing coverage at the earliest possible age is a wise decision.

4. HOW IS YOUR CURRENT HEALTH?

Importance Rating: 5

Your **current health** not only has a direct effect on the premium, but a direct effect on your eligibility for LTC insurance.

Long-term care insurance is a health-qualifying type of insurance, and you must be in reasonably good health to qualify for coverage. While most of the general population qualifies for coverage, there are specific details about your health that will determine your exact premium, including your height and weight, and whether or not you smoke.

Those in good to excellent health will likely qualify for preferred rates. Generally, preferred rates are reserved for people who are average height and weight, are non-smokers, and have not experienced any negative physical or mental health conditions in recent years.

A person with minor health conditions that are well-controlled, such as arthritis without limitations, will likely qualify for coverage, but will be offered a standard premium rate. The difference in premium rates between a preferred premium rate and a standard premium rate averages about 15%.

If you currently have significant health problems, you may have difficulty obtaining LTC insurance. While some smaller, financially lower-rated insurance carriers may accept your application, we advise extreme caution before purchasing coverage from any company that does not pass the carrier evaluation process we outline in *Chapter 12: Choosing the Right Insurance Carrier.*

Recommendation

All things being equal, consider your suitability for LTC insurance while your health is good to excellent.

5. HOW MUCH WILL THE POLICY PAY PER DAY, WEEK, OR MONTH?

Importance Rating: **5**

The **benefit amount** is the ongoing amount of money the insurance company will pay if you have a claim on the policy.

The benefit amount is the most important decision to make in designing LTC insurance coverage. It is also the most influential factor effecting the amount of your premium.

The benefit amount is expressed in a dollar amount per day, week, or month. For example, if you purchased a policy with a daily benefit amount of $150, you would collect about $4,500 per month when you become eligible for benefits, not including inflation adjusted benefits.

Choosing the most appropriate benefit amount is imperative. The *Comprehensive Planning Approach* uses the cost of care in your area as a benchmark. Then, by defining your risk tolerance philosophy, your personal and financial objectives, and your budget, a customized solution is developed by selecting the proper benefit amount for your unique situation. This process analyzes and determines whether to purchase coverage that will pay the full average cost of care, or whether to co-insure by electing coverage that pays for some, but not all of the average cost of care in your area.

In using a benchmark for the cost of care in your area, it's important to use the specific cost of care in your city or immediate area. Do not use the average cost of care in your state because this will not produce accurate results. For example, costs of care in New York State can range from a low of $135 per day to a high of $278 per day.

Recommendation

Most people who purchase LTC insurance later regret that they did not purchase a higher benefit amount. Start by considering a benefit amount that covers the full average cost of care in your area. Then, if applicable, adjust the benefit amount downward based on your risk tolerance philosophy and the amount of money you are budgeting for LTC insurance.

6. HOW LONG WILL THE POLICY PAY BENEFITS?

Importance Rating:

The **maximum lifetime benefit** is the factor that determines the maximum amount of money your LTC insurance policy will pay in dollars once you have a claim and begin to receive benefits. The concept is similar to an accumulated savings account from which you can withdraw money. Once you have a claim, you can withdraw the daily, weekly, or monthly benefit amount explained in number 5 above. Once your maximum lifetime benefit is reached, the policy will pay no further benefits.

The maximum lifetime benefit is chosen when you apply for coverage. As soon as you collect your first dollar of benefits from the policy, it's subtracted from your maximum lifetime benefit.

You can choose a maximum lifetime benefit of as little as one year of long-term care expenses. Or, on the upper end, you can choose a maximum lifetime benefit with "no limit." These two examples are the extremes in the available options; many options exist between these two extremes. As you would presume, the longer the maximum lifetime benefit, the higher the premium.

The no limit choice is also known as the "unlimited benefit maximum," or a "lifetime benefit period." This option allows you to continue collecting benefits for as long as you need care, even if the care is needed for several decades or even for the rest of your life.

The maximum lifetime benefit is one of the most difficult choices to make in designing an LTC insurance policy. Accurate statistics regarding the average duration of long-term care needs are difficult to obtain. There are two major reasons for this:

1. Until the past two decades, there has been little reason for our government or the insurance industry to keep records of how long people need long-term care.

2. When long-term care is needed, people are cared for at home by a loved one, usually a wife or daughter, prior to entering a facility. Statistics regarding the duration of care received at home prior to admission to a facility are extremely difficult to obtain.

By analyzing your family's health history, you may be able to determine how long you might need long-term care services. A longer benefit period may be important if:

- There is longevity in your family.
- There is a history of Alzheimer's Disease or other types of dementia in your family.
- There is a history of neurological conditions, such as Parkinson's Disease in your family.

Recommendation

If you are fortunate enough to be investigating LTC insurance at a fairly young age (under age 65), the difference in premium between the unlimited benefit maximum and a limited benefit maximum is fairly negligible. In this case, the "unlimited benefit maximum" is your best value if the premium is affordable.

If affordability is an issue, consider coverage with a limit that would cover you for 5 to 10 years of care. Recently obtained statistics indicate that the majority of people do not need long-term care for more than 10 years. But never choose a maximum lifetime benefit that pays benefits for less than 5 years of care.

7. WHAT IS THE POLICY ELIMINATION PERIOD?

Importance Rating:

Also known as the deductible, the **elimination period** is similar to deductibles with other types of insurance coverage, such as your automobile or homeowner's insurance. However, instead of being defined as a dollar amount, the elimination period with LTC insurance is defined in *days between the time you begin to need care and the time the policy begins to pay benefits.* For example, if you need long-term care services, and you had purchased coverage with a 100-day elimination period, on the 101st day of your need for care, your elimination period would be satisfied and the policy would begin to pay the benefit amount.

The more days that you are willing to pay for your care out of pocket before your policy begins paying benefits, the lower your premium rate. You can choose a variety of elimination periods, ranging from a zero-day elimination period—which would pay benefits from the first day you needed long-term care services—to elimination periods as high as 730 days or longer.

There are various methods for calculating how the elimination period is satisfied. Some insurance companies use a calendar day method, whereby your elimination period begins on the day you begin to need care and every day counts, even if you do not receive care every subsequent day thereafter. Other companies use a "days of service" method, whereby an elimination period day must be a day that care was actually received. But in the overall picture of LTC insurance policy design, the method used to satisfy the elimination period is a minor consideration.

The elimination period is the most practical way to save money on your premium. Without sacrificing significant benefits, an elimination period in the range of 100 days can save a significant amount of premium dollars over a lower elimination period.

In determining the elimination period most appropriate for your situation and how that translates into out-of-pocket dollars, consider two important points:

1. Your risk tolerance philosophy and whether or not you believe in co-insuring a small or large amount of your potential long-term care costs.

2. The average cost of care in your area. Use this figure to calculate your out-of-pocket dollar risk for various elimination periods by multiplying the elimination period by the average cost of care per day in your area.

Recommendation

We have emphasized many times that *true* long-term care is *needing assistance for a period beyond 100 days*. Short-term care, care needed for less than 100 days, can normally be paid for without significant hardship to the person receiving the care or their family. In certain instances, a percentage of short-term care may be paid for by your health insurance or Medicare. For these reasons, always concentrate your premium dollars on *true* long-term care. This means choosing an elimination period of at least 100 days.

Some people view LTC insurance as a highly catastrophic type of insurance, and choose elimination periods much higher than 100 days—sometimes up to 730 days or more. We caution however, that this strategy could cause unexpected problems: if a policy's benefits cannot be accessed until several months or years after the need for care, a policyholder and their family may be tempted to delay quality caregiving that could have been received earlier.

RIDERS: BELLS AND WHISTLES

Long-term care insurance can be purchased with an array of extra "benefits" that can be added to the basic policy. These bells and whistles are called *riders.*

While these riders increase the premium, most of them fail to add significant value to the coverage. But some are worth considering.

INFLATION PROTECTION

Importance Rating: **5**

The costs of long-term care services will definitely increase in the coming decades. An inflation protection benefit will help hedge against these rising costs. This rider should be an essential part of virtually every LTC insurance policy.

The inflation protection rider automatically raises the benefit amount of your policy each year. Without having to think about it, or pay an increasingly higher premium each year, the rider helps ensure that your LTC Planning objectives continue to be reached.

Long-term care insurance inflation protection riders normally offer a 5% simple or 5% compound inflation benefit. The compound inflation protection benefit is more costly, but is the best choice because it is more realistically tied to probable inflation rates. This means that if your policy has a maximum monthly benefit of $4,000 when you purchase it, in the 13th month of your policy, your monthly benefit will automatically rise to $4,200 per month. The compound inflation rider will double the benefits of your policy every 14 years. If you purchase the simple 5% inflation benefit, your benefits will double every 20 years.

You still need to monitor the rising cost of care in your area to make sure your plan is meeting your objectives. An annual review of your coverage by your LTC Planning and Insurance expert should include a comparison of the new current costs of care with your latest inflation-adjusted benefit amount.

Recommendation

The reason this benefit is included in the riders section of this chapter is because it is possible to purchase LTC insurance without inflation protection. But inflation will always be with us, with a high probability that the inflation rate for long-term care services will be higher over time than the overall economic inflation rate.

For this reason, we recommend the following:

- Everyone who purchases coverage at age 70 and under should purchase the compound inflation protection benefit.
- If you are purchasing coverage between ages 71 and 75, and the compound inflation protection benefit adds too much to the premium, consider the simple inflation protection benefit.
- If you are purchasing coverage after age 75, and both the compound and simple inflation protection benefit riders add too much to the premium, consider increasing your benefit amount to act as a cushion against inflation. It may be more practical at these ages to purchase an additional 25% in benefit amount, for example, rather than an inflation protection benefit. Your LTC Planning and Insurance expert can guide you in this decision.

RESTORATION OF BENEFITS

Importance Rating:

This rider states that if you buy a policy with a "limited benefit maximum" and you use a portion of your policy benefits, the benefits in your policy will be restored if your health returns and you go without care for a specified period of time (usually six months or longer).

Recommendation

The likelihood is low that a person will receive long-term care for more than 100 days, then fully recover, and then later receive care again. This rider is not a good value.

NONFORFEITURE BENEFIT

Importance Rating:

This rider states that if you cancel your LTC insurance policy, a minimal amount of "paid up" insurance will remain in force, to slightly compensate you for premium payments paid to the insurance company. The amount of "paid-up" coverage is normally equal to the cumulative amount of premium you paid. For example, if your annual premium is $3,000, and you canceled the policy after five years, you would have "paid up" coverage of $15,000. The $15,000 would be your maximum lifetime benefit. In this example, if you need care in the future, you could collect the benefit amount, up to a maximum of $15,000.

Recommendation

LTC insurance becomes more valuable the longer it's in force. Only 4% of LTC insurance policyholders have canceled their policies during the first 10 years the policies were in force. This rider is not a good value.

SURVIVORSHIP BENEFIT

Importance Rating:

This rider states that if a couple have coverage with the same company, and one passes away after the policies have been in force for a certain number of years with no claims paid on either policy, the surviving insured's policy will be "paid-up:" No further premium payments would be due. The typical number of years that both policies must be in force and claim-free in order to benefit from this rider is 10 years.

Recommendation

This rider may be a good value if one insured is significantly older than the other. If this is not the case, we recommend that you not spend extra premium dollars on this rider.

SHARED-CARE BENEFIT

Importance Rating:

This rider allows couples who are insured with the same insurance company to use one another's LTC insurance benefits. For example, if a couple purchases "limited benefit" policies, and one insured goes on claim and depletes their benefits but still requires care, this rider would allow them to access the benefits of the other insured's policy.

Recommendation

We recommend first considering the Unlimited Benefit Maximum. Following this recommendation negates the need to spend extra money on the shared care rider.

Couples who are over age 65, and cannot afford the Unlimited Benefit Maximum may consider this rider a good value. If you are older than 65 and applying for coverage with your spouse, ask your LTC Planning and Insurance expert about the feasibility of this option.

GUARANTEED INSURABILITY OPTION

Importance Rating:

This rider, also known as "The Future Purchase Option," allows you to purchase additional LTC insurance in later years, without going through the health-qualifying process again. This means that if you develop a health condition that would normally exclude you from purchasing additional coverage, this rider will allow you to purchase a pre-determined, limited amount of additional coverage in future years.

This benefit normally offers the option to purchase additional coverage at pre-determined intervals during the life of the policy. For example, the insurance company may allow you to exercise this option every two years. This offer would come in the form of a letter from the company, asking you if you would like to exercise the Guaranteed Insurability Option of your policy. If you elect to exercise the option, your premium for the additional coverage will be based on your new "attained age"—not the age at which you initially purchased the policy. But if you have developed new health conditions, you might be glad to have the option to purchase the additional coverage, even at the higher age rate.

Recommendation

Depending on the cost, this can be a worthwhile rider at advanced ages, due to the increased susceptibility for developing health conditions as we age. But if you are under 65, and have been in good to excellent health all your life, we recommend concentrating your premium dollars on purchasing additional "benefit amount" coverage, rather than spending money on this rider. If you are over 65, ask your LTC Planning and Insurance expert about the feasibility of this option.

RETURN OF PREMIUM BENEFIT

Importance Rating:

Upon your death, this rider returns to your beneficiary all or a portion of the premium you paid. If you collect benefits from the policy, the amount returned to your beneficiary will be reduced by the amount you collect due to a claim(s).

Recommendation

This rider adds from 25% to 40% to the basic premium and is not normally a good value. But if you are considering LTC insurance prior to age 50, ask your LTC Planning and Insurance expert to explain the details of this rider to you.

Balancing Act

With a 20-year health career, I have a special place in my heart for older people. After completing my nursing degree, I moved so I could care for my grandmother. What I did not plan on was her son (my uncle) having multiple strokes at the age of 62. So there I was, with a family of my own, including a 5-year old and a 2-year old, caring for a 62-year old and an 85-year old, and still working 10 hour shifts. Within 3 months it became obvious that we could no longer continue with this pace. My family needed more attention, and my health was beginning to be affected by the responsibilities. We declared a state of emergency which allowed my uncle to be admitted into a nursing home. We also moved Grandma into an assisted living arrangement.

These personal experiences motivated me to become an LTC Planning and Insurance expert. I now educate people about the 4 ways to pay or provide for care, and assist people in determining the best option for them and their families. My goal is to help others in the development of a plan, to prevent them from having to "react" to a long-term care need like I did.

— Julia Farman

KEY POINTS

The Essentials of Long-Term Care Insurance

➤ Seven long-term care insurance factors influence the premium. Some of the factors also affect the amount you will receive at the time of claim. Some factors are much more important than others.

➤ Long-term care insurance policies pay benefits under the reimbursement method, indemnity method, or cash method.

➤ Policies are specific as to where you'll receive care: home, facility, or any setting of your choice.

➤ Choose a benefit amount using a benchmark based on the cost of care in your immediate area, not based on the average cost of care in your state.

➤ Of all the policy riders available, the inflation protection rider is the most important benefit to purchase.

Chapter 11

Designing the Right Coverage: A Case Study

Every well-built house started in the form
of a definite purpose plus a definite plan
in the nature of a set of blueprints.

— Napoleon Hill (1883-1970)
American Writer

If LTC insurance is determined to be the best LTC Planning option for you, the next step in the *Comprehensive Planning Approach* is to design coverage customized for your particular situation, and personal and financial objectives. Your financial advisor, estate planning attorney, or CPA should refer you to an LTC Planning and Insurance expert who will assist you in the design of your LTC insurance plan.

DESIGNING A LONG-TERM CARE INSURANCE PLAN

Your LTC Planning and Insurance expert will guide you through six steps:

1. **Review** the analysis that resulted in LTC insurance being your option for planning for long-term care. This analysis is a result of using the first four steps of the *Comprehensive Planning Approach,* explained in *Chapter 7.*

2. **Customize** the coverage. Focus on your current financial situation and personal objectives, your health, and the cost of long-term care in your area. Consider your risk tolerance philosophy, which dictates the ability and willingness to pay for some of your long-term care expenses out-of-pocket. Taking all of these factors into consideration will result in policy benefits that are tailored to your unique situation.

3. **Select** the insurance carrier. Identify the top-rated insurance carriers that offer options within the parameters of the customized coverage determined in Step 2, and select the most appropriate company for you and your family.

4. **Apply** for LTC insurance.

5. **Provide** a copy of your written plan for long-term care and the specific LTC insurance policy benefits to your financial professional(s) and to appropriate family members, if they are not already personally involved in the planning process. This distribution of the details of the plan is a service that should be provided by the LTC Planning and Insurance expert.

6. **Review** the LTC insurance benefits at least annually with your LTC Planning and Insurance expert.

As you can see from Step 5, communication between the LTC Planning and Insurance expert and your financial professional is imperative. This ensures that the LTC Plan you have developed is fully integrated into your financial and estate planning objectives.

A CASE STUDY IN DESIGNING THE RIGHT COVERAGE

The importance of using the *Comprehensive Planning Approach* as opposed to a *single sales approach* is explained throughout this book. The steps in the process are explained in *Chapter 7.*

To illustrate the potential results of these two opposing approaches, the following case study gives a real-life example of a woman who became involved in the LTC insurance purchasing process while we were writing this book. She first worked with an agent using a traditional *single sales approach* and later with an LTC Planning and Insurance expert who is certified in the *Comprehensive Planning Approach*—a professional referred to her by her financial advisor.

For illustrative purposes, we'll call this woman Betty Anderson. Betty was first solicited about LTC insurance by the agent who handles her automobile insurance. Consistent with a *single sales approach,* the agent presented her with options from the standpoint of an insurance sale, rather than from the standpoint of an integrated financial and estate planning solution. **The agent did not:**

- Educate her about the four ways to pay for long-term care
- Educate her about the cost of care in her area
- Discuss her risk tolerance philosophy
- Have any knowledge of her finances and was therefore unable to assist her with an Affordability Analysis to determine how much she could budget for LTC insurance

The objective of the entire approach was to sell insurance, rather than integrate an LTC Plan with the client's personal and financial objectives.

The agent did ask about her health, but only because this is a necessary part of the LTC insurance application process. He learned that Betty had high blood pressure, which meant that the one insurance carrier the agent represented would consider issuing coverage to her, but only at a standard premium rate, not a preferred premium rate.

The agent attempted to persuade her to sign an application during their first conversation about LTC insurance. But she resisted, remembering that her financial advisor had recently mailed her a letter suggesting that they discuss a plan for long-term care during their upcoming review of her financial plan. She took the LTC insurance proposals given to her by the generalist insurance agent to her financial advisor and sought further advice.

Betty's financial advisor was able to educate her about the need to plan ahead for long-term care and answered important basic questions about her options. After doing so, Betty's advisor referred her to an LTC Planning and Insurance expert.

Some Facts About the Client

Before we get into the specific recommendations given by each agent and the potential results of those recommendations, it's important to know some specific details about the client that were learned as a result of using the *Comprehensive Planning Approach.*

Betty is 48 years old. She is in excellent health, other than high blood pressure, which is under good control. She is a divorced mother of twins who have recently graduated from college. There is longevity in her family. Her family also has a history of needing care: her father developed Alzheimer's Disease and needed long-term care beginning at age 76. He received care in an assisted living facility for the final eight years of his life.

Betty owns her own employment agency, which does business as a C-Corporation. Her annual income is $85,000. Her total net worth is $550,000, including liquid assets of about $125,000. She had given little thought to her risk tolerance philosophy with regards to LTC Planning.

The Generalist Insurance Agent's Recommendation

The generalist insurance agent focused his efforts on what he believed Betty could afford to pay for LTC insurance. He based his affordability assumption on what most of his clients who buy coverage can afford to pay.

Since the agent was not integrating an LTC Planning solution within the context of her personal and financial objectives, he had no knowledge of how to assist Betty with understanding:

- **Affordability:** Her specific finances were not discussed, so he simply estimated that Betty could afford a premium of about $2,000 per year.

- **Cost of care in the area:** He had a general idea about the costs of long-term care, but he had no specific knowledge of the average costs of care in Betty's area, which is $120 per day.

- **Risk tolerance philosophy:** He did not offer to assist her in determining her risk tolerance philosophy, which would determine whether or not she should co-insure for some of the potential long-term care costs.

Other vital steps in the *Comprehensive Planning Approach* were also ignored, including answering one of the most important questions of all: How was it determined that LTC insurance may be the best solution for Betty? LTC insurance only makes sense if a process is used that has a person integrating the solution with their objectives and designing the coverage based on an analysis of their personal situation.

The agent made the following plan design recommendations:

- Benefit Amount: $100 per day
- Elimination Period: 0 Days
- Maximum Lifetime Benefit: Lifetime, Unlimited
- Inflation Protection? No
- Guaranteed Insurability Option? Yes
- Underwriting Class: Standard
- Policy Premiums Payable: For Life
- Annual Premium: $1,986
- Effective Premium after Tax Write-off: $1,450

These benefit recommendations are imbalanced and would have resulted in Betty being both over-insured and under-insured, all in the same plan. Let's analyze each specific area:

- **Benefit Amount:** The benefit amount is the most important consideration in LTC insurance policy design. Since the agent is unaware of the average cost of care in her area, he offers no benchmark from which to recommend a benefit amount. He is recommending a low benefit amount for her situation.

- **Elimination Period:** The recommendation of an elimination period of 0 days is not appropriate because *true* long-term care begins after 100 days of care. Betty can probably afford to pay for the first few weeks or months of care herself, but neither Betty nor the agent have discussed the concept of protecting "large dollars." This would normally be discussed during an analysis of her risk tolerance philosophy.

- **Maximum Lifetime Benefit:** The Unlimited Benefit Maximum is a good recommendation.

- **Inflation Protection:** The lack of inflation protection is the most serious mistake made in the policy design recommended by this agent. The odds of needing long-term care are significant beyond age 75. But by the time Betty reaches that age, the policy would pay only a small fraction of the total costs of long-term care. The effects of inflation, and the policy's lack of inflation protection, would cause a significant erosion in her estate at claim's time.

- **Guaranteed Insurability Option:** This rider is best considered for people who are age 65 and older. Betty would be better advised to allocate these premium dollars elsewhere—to purchasing a higher benefit amount and inflation protection, for example.

- **Underwriting Class:** Since the agent only represents one insurance company, he was unable to shop the market and attempt to locate a company that would consider offering Betty a preferred health premium rate.

- **Policy Premiums Payable:** This recommendation has Betty paying LTC insurance premiums for the rest of her life, even during her retirement years. This is appropriate in most cases. But based on the information provided by Betty during the subsequent *Comprehensive Planning Approach* analysis performed by the LTC Planning and Insurance expert, this approach is not in the best interest of her unique situation.

- **Effective Premium After Tax Write-off:** The agent is not aware that Betty can save $536 annually by writing off the premium as a tax deduction. This tax deduction may have been missed if she had worked only with this agent.

Potential Outcome at Claim's Time

This plan design could result in enormous out-of- pocket costs for long-term care. Here is a hypothetical example:

Let's presume that Betty purchased the above policy and followed the path of her father, developing Alzheimer's Disease and entering an assisted living facility at age 76. Let's also presume that, just like her father, she ends up needing care for 8 years. Between the time of purchase and the time of claim, let's presume that inflation has risen at a rate of 5% compounded annually. Let's also presume a very common scenario when it comes to whether or not people exercise the Guaranteed Insurability Option: because of the rising costs of LTC insurance premiums during the years after her policy is issued, Betty elects not to exercise any of the options available to her with regards to the Guaranteed Insurability Option. This means her daily benefit remains at $100 per day.

Here is the cost/benefit scenario for Betty at age 76, when her hypothetical claim begins:

- The original cost of care in her area was $120 per day. But the effects of inflation and the lack of inflation protection will be financially devastating to Betty at claim's time. The cost of care in her area at the time of need, due to a 5% compounding inflation rate, will have quadrupled to $480 per day!

- The policy will begin to pay for care from the first day of need, due to the recommendation of a zero-day elimination period.

- The 8 year duration of care equates to 2,920 days. Using the daily cost of care of $480, the total long-term care bill would come to just under $1.4 million.

- The policy would pay for 2,920 days of care at a rate of $100 per day. The total benefit paid by the policy for those 8 years of care would be $292,000.

- The out-of-pocket expenses to Betty would be over $1.1 million!

Even though a claim of this nature would have Betty paying only $56,000 in premiums for a return of $292,000 in benefits, the improper coverage design would fail to meet her personal and financial objectives, and would cause her to lose a large portion of her assets. This devastating impact to her financial security would be entirely due to the inappropriate plan design that often results from using a *single sales approach*.

The LTC Planning and Insurance Expert's Recommendation

Before meeting with Betty, the agent certified in the *Comprehensive Planning Approach* consulted with her financial advisor to learn about Betty's situation and objectives. This assures that the LTC Plan will be integrated with her financial plan.

During her first meeting with Betty, this agent continued to educate her about the issues of long-term care that were not specifically discussed by the financial advisor. These areas included the specific cost of care in her area, an analysis of her risk tolerance philosophy, an Affordability Analysis, and an analysis of her personal and financial objectives as they related to a potential need for long-term care.

This agent supported her facts about the cost of care in the area ($120 per day) with information from various assisted living communities and home care providers in the area.

After becoming further educated about the issue of long-term care, and how it relates to her risk tolerance philosophy, Betty came to understand that her philosophy is to protect "large dollars." She was not interested in protecting relatively small amounts of money, and was willing to pay for short-term care herself.

The effects of inflation were discussed, and the LTC Planning and Insurance expert emphasized that designing LTC coverage at age 48 without inflation protection would be foolish. The agent informed Betty that inflation rates for long-term care expenses were currently around 3.5%, but that this rate was predicted to double in future years, and would likely average at least 5% over time.

The agent also gathered information about Betty's health, but went beyond the basic information needed for an application. She asked for more specific information about Betty's high blood pressure, and learned that it had been well-controlled for almost six years.

Since the agent is independently licensed with a number of top-rated companies, she was able to search for a company that would offer Betty preferred rates, based on the fact that her blood pressure is under good control. This would save Betty about 15% in premium over the standard health rating offered by the first and only carrier represented by the agent using the *single sales approach.*

The agent also learned about Betty's retirement goals: She planned to work for about 15 more years, and would sell her company at the time of retirement.

Determining how much she could afford to pay for the premium was an important aspect of the process. But even more important was creating coverage designed to accomplish the results that are important to Betty. During the Affordability Analysis, Betty learned that she had an opportunity to tax deduct the premium for her coverage through her corporation. She also learned that she had the opportunity to purchase LTC insurance that could be "paid up" by the time she reached her retirement years.

The thorough process of the *Comprehensive Planning Approach* helped Betty integrate her plan for long-term care within the context of her personal and financial objectives.

After the analysis, the LTC Planning and Insurance expert made the following plan design recommendations:

- Benefit Amount: $120 per day
- Elimination Period: 100 days
- Maximum Lifetime Benefit: Lifetime, Unlimited
- Inflation Protection: Yes
- Guaranteed Insurability Option: No

- Underwriting Class: Preferred
- Policy Premiums Payable: For 10 years
- Annual Premium: $3,511
- Effective Premium After Tax Write-off: $2,563

These recommendations offer a customized result that comes much closer to ensuring that Betty will achieve her desired objectives.

Let's analyze each specific area:

- **Benefit Amount:** The recommended benefit amount used an accurate benchmark and pays for the average cost of care in her area today.

- **Elimination Period:** Betty saves premium dollars by choosing a comfortable elimination period. She will pay for "short-term care" herself—the first 100 days of care.

- **Maximum Lifetime Benefit:** The policy will pay benefits for as long as the coverage is needed.

- **Inflation Protection:** Adding the inflation protection benefit is the most significant difference between the recommendations given by the two agents. This benefit offers a hedge against the most serious threat to a solid LTC Plan—inflation.

- **Guaranteed Insurability Option:** This rider is not recommended to Betty at her age because most young people never exercise this option. It makes more sense to use these premium dollars to purchase a higher benefit amount and inflation protection.

- **Underwriting Class:** Because this agent is independently licensed with several top-rated companies, Betty received the benefit of having the agent "shop" for a company that would offer her a preferred health premium rate.

- **Policy Premiums Payable:** After learning about Betty's goal of retiring in 15 years, this agent recommended a policy that would have her paying no premiums during her retirement years.

- **Annual Premium:** Because the policy premium is payable for only 10 years instead of for life, the premium for this policy is higher than the policy that requires premium payments for life. But the Affordability Analysis made Betty realize that she could afford the extra premium and that it was worth the pay-off of having no LTC insurance premiums in retirement.

- **Effective Premium After Tax Write-off:** Betty and her CPA are informed that since she owns a C-Corporation, she can tax deduct the premium and her effective premium rate is reduced by $948.

Potential Outcome at Claim's Time

The potential outcome of this more customized recommendation will allow Betty to receive benefits at claim's time that will preserve much more of her estate. The plan is fully integrated with her personal and financial objectives and considers the future inflationary conditions that will affect her cost of care in the years ahead.

Using the same scenario of needing care for eight years beginning at age 76, this customized plan design would have the following outcome at the time of claim:

- The cost of care in her area is now $480 per day. Due to the inclusion of the inflation protection rider, the policy would pay the entire cost of care.

- The elimination period of 100 days means that Betty pays for the first 100 days herself. This equates to $48,000 in out-of-pocket expenses at the beginning of the need for care.

- The policy would pay benefits for 2,820 days (8 years, minus the 100 days paid by Betty) for a total policy benefit payout of $1.35 million.

SUMMARY

By customizing coverage using the *Comprehensive Planning Approach,* Betty's policy would pay an extra $1 million in benefits over the policy recommended as a result of using a *single sales approach.*

The above example is a real life example of someone who worked with 2 agents using 2 opposing approaches to LTC insurance plan design. The example is for illustrative purposes only from the standpoint of the hypothetical claims.

Regardless of the benefits you choose, review your plan at least annually, to ensure that it accomplishes the desired results.

CASE STUDY: SUMMARY OF PLAN DESIGNS AND POTENTIAL RESULTS

	The Comprehensive Planning Approach	*A Single Sales Approach*
Education and Advice	Thorough understanding of long-term care including: • Implications of relying on four ways to pay for long-term care • Cost of care in area • Analysis of risk tolerance philosophy • Affordability analysis	Limited. Emphasis on selling LTC insurance
Integration with Personal and Financial Objectives	Major Emphasis	Minor Emphasis
Carrier Comparison	Several top-rated carriers	None
Underwriting Class	Preferred	Standard
Benefit Amount	$120 per day	$100 per day
Elimination Period	100 days	0 days
Maximum Lifetime Benefit	Lifetime, Unlimited	Lifetime, Unlimited
Inflation Protection	Yes	No
Guaranteed Insurability Option	No	Yes
Policy Premiums Payable	For 10 Years	For Life
Annual Premium	$3,511	$1,986
Effective Premium After Tax Write-off	$2,563	$1,450
Cumulative Premium Paid at Hypothetical Claim's Time	$35,110	$55,608
Hypothetical Policy Benefit Payout	$1.35 Million	$292,000
Hypothetical Out-of-Pocket Expenses	$48,000	$1.1 Million

KEY POINTS

Designing the Right Coverage: A Case Study

➤ Carefully consider the premium/benefit trade-off to make sure your premium dollars are used to customize coverage that is well balanced and is likely to result in achieving your personal and financial objectives.

➤ For the most appropriate long-term care insurance plan design, consult with a financial advisor who refers you to an LTC Planning and Insurance expert certified in the *Comprehensive Planning Approach.*

Chapter 12

Choosing the Right Insurance Carrier

We cannot direct the wind but we can adjust the sails.

— Vince Lombardi

Choosing the right LTC insurance carrier is the most important consideration in the LTC insurance planning process. All the other details of coverage, including benefits, premium rates, tax advantages and more, are irrelevant if you choose the wrong insurance company. At the time of claim, the depth of commitment, integrity, and financial strength of the insurance company is what matters most.

COMMITMENT TO THE MARKET

The Introduction to Part 3, *"History of the LTC Insurance Industry,"* offers a chronology of the industry and describes the problems that can arise when insurance carriers enter an area of risk that the carriers have not fully researched.

In recent years, a record number of insurance companies that had entered the LTC insurance market in the mid-1990s have exited the market. Companies that exit the market must, by law, honor their commitment to current policyholders, by keeping their coverage in force and paying claims.

Since an insurance company must honor all its existing policies even if it exits the market, it would seem that selecting the right insurance carrier would simply be a matter of choosing the company with the best benefits and the lowest premium. However, an insurance company will only remain in markets that are profitable for the company. If a company exits the LTC insurance market, the likelihood is very high that they **did not** understand the market, and as a result underpriced premiums and issued coverage with underwriting standards that were too liberal. To compensate, the insurance company will begin to impose frequent and sometimes substantial rate increases on its existing policyholders. These

FAST FACTS:

■ Reasonableness in premium rates is an important consideration in selecting the proper carrier. Reasonable premium rates mean not too high or too low.

■ A stringent underwriting process is an indication of a carrier that will remain committed to the market.

■ Consider insurance carriers that have been in the long-term care insurance market for **10 years or longer.**

■ Choose one of the larger, more diversified LTC insurance carriers.

policyholders may suddenly find that what was initially the lowest premium on the market is now the highest. Since a high percentage of these existing policies have been in force for years, many policyholders will have developed health conditions that prohibit them from obtaining coverage from another insurance carrier. Their choices are now severely limited: risk paying an increasingly higher premium in the future, or cancel the coverage and go without the insurance protection they had planned to use to pay for their long-term care expenses.

EVALUATING INSURANCE CARRIERS

History proves that most insurance companies that enter the LTC insurance market will not remain in the market for an extended period of time. Therefore, the majority of insurance companies offering LTC insurance should be avoided. Narrow your choice of companies to those that are highly committed to the industry, have a history of excellent premium stability, and have published their claim's payment history. Following are guidelines for selecting such companies.

Longevity in the Long-Term Care Insurance Industry

The longer a company has been in the LTC insurance business, the more likely they are to remain in the business. As a general rule, it's best to select an insurance company that has been in the market for 10 years or longer. Avoid companies that enter the market, exit the market, and then re-enter the market again. This indicates a lack of commitment to the LTC insurance industry.

Financial Ratings

Don't believe the myth that insurance company financial ratings are not important. To the contrary, a strong financial rating is **vital** to the future of your investment in the coverage.

If you are in excellent health you should select a company with an **A Plus** rating by the A.M. Best financial rating service. If you have minor health conditions and cannot obtain coverage with such a company, consider coverage with an **A** rated company. *Never* choose an insurance company rated less than **A** by A.M. Best.

Although A.M. Best is one of the oldest and most respected financial rating services, you may also want to ask your LTC Planning and Insurance expert about a company's financial rating with one of the other rating services listed at the end of this chapter.

Name Recognition of the Insurance Company

Recognizing the name of the insurance company is another indicator that the company will remain committed to the market. Insurance companies that have built name recognition and have protected a brand name over a number of decades are more likely to continue protecting the reputation of the company name. The large name brand companies rarely make short-term decisions, such as entering a market without first researching it thoroughly. While small companies *may* be a safe place to invest your LTC insurance premium dollars, why take the chance? Choose one of the larger, well-recognized names in the insurance industry.

Approved as a "Partnership" Company

In *Chapter 16,* we explain that "Partnership" LTC insurance companies are superior to non-Partnership companies. Companies that have been approved as a "Partnership" company have gone through a stringent approval process that indicates a major commitment to the LTC insurance industry. Regardless of whether a Partnership program is available in your state, narrow your insurance company selection to companies that have been Partnership approved. Partnership companies offer traditional LTC insurance in most states and choosing one of these companies offers better odds for rate stability and a smooth claim's payment experience.

Rate Increase History

Long-term care insurance premium rates can be increased on existing policies if an insurance carrier can justify the rate increase to your state's insurance department. Since policies are subject to rate increases, always ask about the rate increase history of the insurance carrier being recommended. Some excellent insurance carriers have done such a good job with underwriting and pricing that no premium rate increases have ever been issued on existing policyholders. Choose one of these top-rated carriers.

Reasonableness in Premium

Choosing a company that has a lower-than-average premium rate could spell disaster for your future LTC insurance plan. This is one of the few industries in which shopping for the lowest price, combined with the most generous benefits, is not a wise decision.

Why should you be concerned about a company with a lower-than-average premium rate? Since no company operates in a vacuum, insurance carriers with rates lower than the average market premium will raise rates substantially in future years.

It also wouldn't be wise to purchase coverage from an insurance carrier with substantially higher than average premium rates. "Reasonableness in premium rates" is the best approach to selecting an insurance carrier you can trust.

Ask your LTC Planning and Insurance expert to show you premium rates from several companies. A general guideline is that the company being recommended should have premium rates that are within 15% of the other top-rated carriers.

Stringent Underwriting Process

Underwriting is the "process of examining, accepting, or rejecting insurance risks, and then classifying those accepted in order to charge the proper amount of premium" *(National Association of Insurance Commissioners)*.

For people in good to excellent health, it's best to select an insurance carrier with a rigorous underwriting process. Since you have maintained your good health, you should be rewarded by being insured in a "risk pool" of people who have also maintained their good health. Doing business with an insurance carrier with a conservative underwriting philosophy is the best strategy for keeping your premium rate stable in future years. A stringent underwriting process is your strongest indication that the insurance carrier will also be in a good position to pay your claim in the future and will be less likely to substantially raise your rates along the way.

Unfortunately, a rigorous underwriting process is not good for people in poor health. But people in poor health are very fortunate if they can obtain LTC insurance at all. Current trends in underwriting with all quality carriers indicate that people with health problems will soon be unable to obtain long-term care insurance.

FINANCIAL RATING SERVICES

A.M. Best
Ambest Rd.
Oldwick, NJ 08858
908-439-2200
www.ambest.com

Provides ratings for insurance companies. No charge for company ratings. Full written reports are available for $35 per report. Free rating information is available via the company's website.

Demotech, Inc.
2941 Donnylane Blvd.
Columbus, OH 43235
1-800-354-7207
www.demotech.com

Provides financial stability ratings for insurance companies. There is a small fee to the insurance company being rated; information is free to consumers. Information needed: insurance company name. Free rating information is available via the company's website.

Fitch
55 E. Monroe St., Suite 3500
Chicago, IL 60603
1-800-853-4824
www.fitchratings.com

Provides ratings for 1–5 insurance companies over the phone at no charge. Information needed: insurance company name. A fee is charged to the insurance company being rated. Free rating information is available via the website.

Moody's Investors Services
99 Church St.
New York, NY 10007
212-553-0377
www.moodys.com

Provides ratings for 1–5 insurance companies per call at no charge. Information needed: insurance company name. Rating information is available via the company's website.

Standard and Poor's Corporation
55 Water St.
New York, NY 10041
212-438-2400
212-208-1527
www.standardandpoors.com/ratings

Provides ratings for 1–5 insurance companies per call at no charge. Information needed: insurance company name. There is a small fee to the insurance company being rated. Free rating information is available via the company's website.

Weiss Research, Inc.
4176 Burns Rd., P.O. Box 109665
Palm Beach Gardens, FL 33410
1-800-289-9222
www.weissratings.com

Provides ratings for insurance companies. There is a $15 charge for a verbal rating (over the phone) for one company.

KEY POINTS

Choosing the Right Insurance Carrier

➤ Choosing the right insurance carrier is the most important consideration in the long-term care insurance planning process.

➤ An insurance carrier must honor all existing policies for as long as premium payments are paid, even if the company exits the long-term care insurance market.

➤ Consider insurance companies that have been in the long-term care insurance market for at least 10 years.

➤ Never choose an insurance company rated less than **"A"** by A.M. Best.

➤ Choose one of the larger, well-recognized companies in the insurance industry.

➤ Narrow your insurance company selection to a "Partnership" company. "Partnership" companies have made a major commitment to the LTC insurance industry, increasing your odds of rate stability and a smooth claim's payment experience.

➤ Choose an insurance carrier that issues coverage with a rigorous and stringent underwriting process.

➤ Ask your LTC Planning and Insurance expert to show you the rate increase history of the company they are recommending.

Chapter 13

The Application and Underwriting Process

Happiness is nothing more than good health and a bad memory.
— Albert Schweitzer (1875-1965)

If the *Comprehensive Planning Approach* determines that LTC insurance is the best planning option for you, the next step is to apply for coverage. The following information explains the process for applying for coverage, and what to expect in the underwriting process:

- **Complete the application.** The application includes personal information such as your name, date of birth, height, and weight. But more importantly, the application includes a series of health questions. The answers to these health questions, and the remainder of the process explained below, will determine whether or not you will be issued coverage, and if so, the exact premium rate you will pay.

  The application and a refundable deposit (usually one month's premium) are submitted to the insurance company's underwriting department. The underwriting department reviews the information on the application.

- **Wait for the decision.** The insurance company may simply issue or decline the policy based on the information on the application. Although it has been common for underwriting to be this simple in the past, the underwriting process today is generally more complex and requires additional steps.

- **Verification of information on your application.** A common step is a telephone conversation between a member of the company's underwriting department and the applicant, to verify the information on the application. A second purpose of the call is to confirm that the applicant understands the type of coverage and benefit amounts for which he or she has applied.

- **Complete a physical exam.** The underwriter may also request a face-to-face physical. While it is becoming more routine for companies to request physical exams, most companies still limit this request to applicants above certain ages, usually age 65. Physical exams on younger applicants may be randomly requested.

  During the physical exam, a memory test for cognitive impairment will also be performed. This is a simple test, designed to assure that a person is not already developing memory problems at the time of application.

  The physical exam is paid for by the insurance company, and is scheduled at a place and time that is convenient for the applicant. No disrobing is required.

> **FAST FACTS:**
>
> ■ Physical exams are commonly performed on applicants 65 and older. The exam is paid for by the insurance company.
>
> ■ The underwriter may request a written statement from your doctor or your actual medical records.
>
> ■ If your application is declined with one company, you may have alternative options with other companies.

- **Request your medical records.** A final step in the underwriting process may include a request for a statement of your health from your doctor, and/or a copy of your medical records.

Based on the results of the information above, the underwriting department of the insurance company will determine whether or not to issue coverage. If coverage is to be issued, your health rating will be determined, which will dictate your exact premium amount. This means that the premium rate quoted by your LTC Planning and Insurance expert may be revised. The quotes provided by these professionals are based on "general underwriting guidelines," using the preliminary information you provide to them about your health. While the premium amount quoted at the time of application is usually accurate, the underwriting process must be completed prior to knowing the exact premium rate.

When the policy is issued, the LTC Planning and Insurance expert will review the details of the coverage and the final premium amount.

You have 30 days to decide whether or not to accept the policy—this is called the "free-look period." This 30-day period begins on the date you actually receive the policy. If you decide not to accept the policy within this 30-day period, the insurance company must refund the initial deposit submitted with the application and the policy is null and void. If you agree to the conditions of the policy, including the final premium amount, the coverage will go into force.

If you accept the policy, you will be asked to select the frequency of your premium payments. Premium payments to the insurance company can be made on an annual, semi-annual, quarterly, or monthly basis. Generally, discounts are available for selecting longer durations between premium payments.

If your application is declined with one insurance company, there may be options to obtain coverage with alternative insurance companies. Your LTC Planning and Insurance expert will assist you in evaluating these options.

KEY POINTS

The Application and Underwriting Process

➤ The underwriting process may involve simply completing an application. But more than likely, additional steps will be taken prior to issuance or denial of the application.

➤ The underwriting process must be completed in order to know the exact final premium rate.

➤ The "free-look period" gives you 30 days to decide whether or not to accept the policy once it is approved and received.

➤ Generally, discounts are available for selecting longer durations between premium payments.

Chapter 14 — Submitting A Claim

Old age is not so bad when you consider the alternatives.
— Maurice Chevalier, *Actor*

Like all insurance coverage, LTC insurance is coverage you hope to never use. But if a long-term care need does arise, you'll certainly appreciate having taken the time to plan ahead. It will then be time to collect benefits from the investment you made in the coverage.

HOW DO YOU BECOME ELIGIBLE FOR BENEFITS?

As with all types of insurance, LTC insurance pays benefits when an "insurable event" occurs. The insurable event with life insurance, for example, would be the death of the insured. The insurable event with an LTC insurance policy has to do with "needing assistance."

Specifically, there are two ways to become eligible for benefits with LTC insurance: Inability to perform ADLs and/or cognitive impairment.

Inability to Perform ADLs

People who need long-term care services have lost their ability to live independently. This is often due to their inability to perform some of the

> ## ADLs
>
> People who have lost their ability to perform activities of daily living, also known as **ADLs**, may require long-term care services.
>
> **ADLs include:**
> - Bathing
> - Dressing
> - Toileting
> - Continence
> - Transferring (from bed to chair, etc.)
> - Eating

activities of daily living, also known as ADLs. *Chapter 1* explained that the need for assistance with ADLs can result from the frailty of aging, a deteriorating health condition(s), or an accident.

The ADL list shown above is in the order in which we typically lose them. This is the reverse order in which we learn them from birth.

FAST FACTS:

- There are two ways to become eligible for benefits: 1) The inability to perform ADLs and/or 2) Cognitive impairment.

- Care Coordinators are independent of both insurance carriers and direct-care providers, so they can be objective and unbiased.

- Care Coordinators recommend care based on the insured's needs and develop a plan of care that coordinates available services.

At the time of claim, an ADL assessment will be performed to determine the extent of your inability to function without assistance.

Recommendation

The best policies pay benefits if you are unable to perform two or more ADLs without assistance. *Never* consider a policy that requires you to need assistance with more than two ADLs to become eligible for benefits. Especially beware of "tricky" policies that require you to lose two ADLs to collect benefits for a nursing home confinement but require three or more ADL deficiencies in order to collect benefits for home care or care in an Assisted Living Community.

Cognitive Impairment

If loss of short-term or long-term memory or other cognitive impairment—such as judgment relating to safety—are severe enough that a person can no longer live independently, the policyholder may be eligible for benefits. Cognitive impairment can "trigger" benefits regardless of whether or not the policyholder is able to perform ADLs. Conditions such as the onset of Alzheimer's Disease are included in this category of cognitive impairment. If this is the reason for the need for care, a cognitive assessment will be performed to determine the extent of the condition.

If the ADL and/or cognitive impairment assessment determines that you are eligible for benefits, a "plan of care" is developed. This is such an important part of the process that we explain it in detail later in this chapter, under Care Coordination.

If you become eligible for benefits, some policies pay benefits for "homemaking services" such as cooking, cleaning, and running errands. These services fall under the category of "Incidental Activities of Daily Living," or IADLs.

Clarification: You cannot receive IADL services unless you first become eligible for benefits by either losing your ability to perform ADLs, or by being cognitive impaired. LTC insurance will not pay for someone to clean, cook, and run errands for you unless you first become eligible for benefits by "triggering" an insurable event.

POLICY EXCLUSIONS

All insurance policies contain exclusions. Exclusions are conditions or circumstances which will prevent a policyholder from collecting benefits from the policy, even if they would have otherwise qualified for benefits.

Typical exclusions found in most LTC insurance policies include:

* Treatment or services for which no charge was made, with the exception of a cash method policy *(see Chapter 10: The Essentials of Long-Term Care Insurance).*
* Care provided or paid for by another type of coverage. For example, if Medicare or your regular health insurance paid for your care, your LTC insurance policy would not normally pay additional benefits. Remember, Medicare, Medicare supplement insurance, or your regular health insurance do not pay for *true* long-term care—care provided beyond 100 days. But if you choose an elimination period of less than 100 days on your LTC insurance policy, and one of these other sources *does* pay for your care during that time, your LTC insurance policy would not normally pay additional benefits.
* War or acts of war.
* Alcoholism or drug addiction.
* Self-inflicted injuries or attempted suicide.

Beware of Mental Exclusion Clause

Some LTC insurance policies contain an exclusion that states that mental and nervous disorders will not be covered, unless the disorder is **"Organically Demonstrable."** Most states have banned this exclusion in policies being issued today, but read the policy exclusions section of any policy being recommended to make sure this clause is not included. **Avoid any policy that contains an exclusion of any kind for mental or nervous disorders.**

THE CLAIM'S PROCESS

The claim's process requires that information from three sources be provided to the insurance company: information from the policyholder, information from the provider (home care provider or facility), and information from the policyholder's physician. It's important that the information from these three sources be consistent or the claim may be delayed or denied. The last problem you and your family need to deal with at claim's time is a clerical error that delays payment of your claim.

SEEK ASSISTANCE WITH THE CLAIM'S PROCESS

The LTC Planning and Insurance expert who works with you when the LTC insurance policy is issued should always be available to assist you and your family in the claim's process. Prior to purchasing coverage, ask for evidence, in writing, of policyholders who have been assisted in the claim's process. Ask for specific references of those who have received assistance, including phone numbers, and permission to call the policyholders. Take the time to call these people who have had claims and received assistance. If the agent cannot supply you with such information, do not do business with this person. Someone who cannot provide you with references of people who have had claims and received claim's assistance should not be attempting to assist you with LTC Planning and Insurance.

WHAT IF YOUR CLAIM IS DENIED?

If the claim's process is handled properly, the likelihood of a legitimate claim being denied is rare. Most states have passed laws mandating high penalties for insurance companies that deny a legitimate claim. LTC Planning and Insurance experts certified in the *Comprehensive Planning Approach* are aware of these laws. Their assistance with your claim will be extra assurance that the insurance company will not deny a legitimate claim.

However, if you feel a legitimate claim has been denied, contact your state insurance department to file a complaint.

CARE COORDINATION

Care Coordination is a value-added benefit that provides assistance to family members at the critical time of the need for care. Care Coordination is defined as *a service that helps manage the coordination of a person's care among all the parties involved.* These parties may include the people currently in the policyholder's circle of support: a spouse, children, and other close relatives, neighbors, and friends. It may also include paid caregivers, facilities, health care practitioners, and social workers. Care Coordinators are health care practitioners who are able to assess the individual needs of a person in need of care, identify the type(s) of care needed, and assist the family in obtaining the care they need.

One of the major benefits of using a Care Coordinator is to benefit from their experience in the practical aspects of long-term care. For example, the Care Coordinator is familiar with long-term care providers in the area, so their service may reduce the time it takes a family and policyholder to screen and select qualified provider(s) that fit the personal needs of the policyholder. This allows family members to provide emotional support to the person in need of care, instead of spending their time researching and interviewing potential providers.

A Care Coordinator is sometimes known as a *Care Manager.* But Care Coordination should not be confused with "managed care." Care Coordinators are not "gatekeepers" to services and/or providers *(for more specifics on the difference, see "Long-Term Care Coordinators: An Interview with Health Care Experts" later in this chapter).*

The Care Coordination process involves two main steps:

1. **Conduct a Comprehensive Assessment.** Visit and interview the person needing care to evaluate their needs. This evaluation may include a physical and cognitive assessment, assessment of social and emotional state of mind, functional capabilities, and living arrangements. The person's circle of support should be available during this assessment.

This thorough assessment allows the Care Coordinator to evaluate the current resources available and link the policyholder to a full range of appropriate services.

2. **Develop a Plan of Care.** The information from the assessment is used to develop a **plan of care** which describes the formal and informal needs to be addressed, the frequency and duration of care, and the cost of care. This **plan of care** should be developed with the participation of the policyholder, the policyholder's family, and the policyholder's physician.

The plan of care is a formal description which specifies the following information:

- The type(s) of care needed
- Where the care can be received
- How much the care will cost
- A recommendation of providers of care
- Any other available alternatives

Care Coordinators may perform other services such as:

- Contact care providers chosen by the insured to initiate services
- Negotiate service provider rates
- Assist with initial claim's forms
- Provide the certification required to satisfy potential requirements from the doctor
- Provide ongoing monitoring of the quality of services provided and provide reassessment of the plan of care as needed
- Development of transitional plans, such as providing assistance to a person who must be moved from their home to an assisted living community
- Document and maintain records
- Intervene during a crisis
- Manage nutrition and diet
- Coordinate bill-paying services

LTC INSURANCE POLICIES ENHANCED
WITH CARE COORDINATION BENEFIT

The Care Coordination benefit is included in some LTC insurance policies. Be sure to confirm that any policy you consider includes the Care Coordination benefit. All other aspects being equal, LTC insurance policies that offer a Care Coordination benefit are superior to policies that do not offer Care Coordination. In addition to relieving family members of the burden of trying to locate quality caregivers, the Care Coordination benefit may also result in better utilization of the benefits of an LTC insurance policy. The LTC insurance benefits may actually be extended or used more efficiently with a plan that coordinates informal and formal care.

LONG-TERM CARE COORDINATORS:
AN INTERVIEW WITH HEALTH CARE EXPERTS

Featured Experts:

- **Susan Westerman,** *HIA (Claims Manager)* and
- **Pat Pannone, RN, BSN, MPH, CMC** *(Care Coordination Manager)* with ERC Long-Term Care Solutions, Third Party Administrator and LTCI Reinsure

This is a paraphrased interview conducted by Jesse R. Slome, CLU, ChFC, Publisher/Editor in Chief, Long-Term Care Insurance Sales Strategies Magazine, Vol. 4, No. 4, www.ltcsales.com and reprinted with permission (Slome 2002).

SLOME: Why are some people concerned when they hear about the Care Coordination benefit of an LTC insurance policy?

PANNONE: It's natural to be concerned because many associate the LTC insurance coordination benefit with medical case management common to health insurance. Many people have experienced a hospitalization where they were introduced to someone called a case manager who basically is a discharge planner. Or, they've had contact with a case manager associated with their health insurer who is in a utilization review role. These functions are distinctly different from the geriatric Care Coordinator's role associated with LTC insurance. But, it is natural for consumers to be unfamiliar or initially uncomfortable with the process of Care Coordination because of the similarity with the term "care management."

SLOME: So, the Care Coordination component of LTC insurance is different. How so?

PANNONE: Long-term care insurance Care Coordination is a benefit to the insured, and is stated as such in the policy. It is a consumer-focused service that links and coordinates assistance from both formal and family/community service providers. The goal is to enable policyholders with chronic functional and/or cognitive limitations to reach optimal independence for their conditions.

The coordinator has special long-term care experience and knowledge and can guide chronically ill people and their families to needed care. They are licensed health care professionals such as a registered nurse or medical social worker. They are skilled in conducting a face-to-face "best practice" comprehensive assessment. They work with both the insured and family members to develop a needs-based plan of care, arrange services, monitor and revise the plan over time, and periodically complete a face-to-face reassessment. The coordinator who meets with the insured can also complete certification of the individual as being chronically ill.

Care Coordinators are independent of both insurance carriers and direct care providers, so they can be as objective and unbiased as possible. They do not determine or pay benefits. The claim analyst interprets the policy and determines benefits based upon the Care Coordinator's recommendations.

SLOME: When is the Care Coordinator engaged?

WESTERMAN: From the beginning of the need for care. Typically, a spouse or family member calls the administrator at the insurance company to file a claim. The administrator arranges for the Care Coordinator to contact the insured for a face-to-face assessment appointment. The initial assessment is typically done at the insured's home, but at the request of the policyholder and family, the visit could take place in any setting. The assessment is done at a time that is convenient to the insured and family members who wish to be present.

SLOME: If you were paying for these Care Coordination services on an independent basis, what would it cost?

PANNONE: A geriatric Care Coordinator/Care Manager typically charges anywhere from $85 to $100 an hour, depending upon expertise and region of the country. So the total cost of these services, including assessment, development of the plan of care, monitoring, and periodic on-site reassessment could cost several hundred dollars a year.

WESTERMAN: And, it's important to note that the cost of Care Coordination is part of the LTC insurance benefit. It's an incredibly valuable benefit for the LTC insurance policyholder.

SLOME: Do Care Coordinators know the provisions of the claimant's LTC insurance policy?

PANNONE: Not prior to the initial assessment. They recommend care based on the insured's needs, regardless of the policy benefits. But if the Care Coordinator learns that there is a recommended setting or type of care not covered under the insured's policy, the Care Coordinator may assist in creating an alternate plan of care as the policy allows, or find other cost-conscious alternatives to preserve the insured's resources.

SLOME: Can you share an example of how a Coordinator assisted an insured and their family?

PANNONE: One major role of the Care Coordinator is to support family caregivers, so that fatigue and burnout doesn't lead to the insured's premature move to a facility.

One case we recently worked on involved an overwhelmed 81-year-old woman caring for her husband with Parkinson's and heart problems. He had ADL deficiencies with bathing and dressing, and also was memory-impaired. They didn't want to have strangers come to their home. The Coordinator recommended they consider an adult day center, explaining the available local resources that could help their situation.

In some cases, the Coordinator might also recommend safety bars in the bathroom or a life-call system. If the insured requires a skilled-care facility, the Coordinator may arrange viable ways to have the individual return home as soon as possible to receive care.

Care Coordination is a benefit that the policyholder can receive during the elimination period. The Care Coordinator often works with the insured or family members during the elimination period to find options that could be less costly. Using this benefit during the elimination period is a valuable aspect of an LTC insurance policy that goes beyond the normal benefits of the coverage.

KEY POINTS

Submitting A Claim

➤ The best long-term care insurance policies pay benefits if you are unable to perform two ADLs.

➤ Policy exclusions that normally prevent a policyholder from collecting benefits include treatment for services for which no charge was made, and self-inflicted injuries.

➤ Your LTC Planning and Insurance expert should assist in the claim's process. Ask for references of people who have placed claims and received claim's assistance.

➤ Care Coordination is a service that includes coordinating a person's care among all the parties involved.

➤ The Care Coordination benefit of an LTC insurance policy may help in better utilizing the policy's benefits. A coordinated plan for efficiently utilizing informal and formal care may actually extend the policy benefits.

➤ LTC insurance policies that offer Care Coordination are superior to policies that do not offer Care Coordination.

PART 4

Incentives To Purchase Long-Term Care Insurance

*The aging process has you
firmly in its grasp if you never
get the urge to throw a snowball.*

— Doug Larson

PART 4:
Incentives to Purchase
Long-Term Care Insurance

As our government, employers, professional organizations and financial institutions begin to fully recognize the coming long-term care crisis, we will see more incentives to plan ahead for long-term care.

Incentives for planning ahead with LTC insurance are currently available through tax advantages, state-sponsored Partnership Programs, and group and sponsored LTC insurance plans offered through employers, associations, financial institutions and other groups. The advantages and disadvantages of these incentive programs are explained in the following three chapters.

Chapter 15

Tax Advantages of Long-Term Care Insurance

I feel very honored to pay taxes in America.
The thing is, I could probably feel
just as honored for about half the price.
— Arthur Godfrey

A year rarely passes without our federal and state governments experiencing budgetary constraints. Our country's budgetary challenges will intensify and worsen as the aging population grows and life expectancies increase.

The federal government continues to commission studies to research ways to finance the long-term care needs of our current senior population, and especially the 76 million aging baby boomers. But there is a pervasive fear among legislators that most Americans do not understand that public programs cannot be relied upon to pay for long-term care. Federal and state governments are actively sending strong signals that public funds to pay for the costs of long-term care will be reduced in the years ahead.

Our legislators are convinced that LTC insurance must play a key role in our country's solution to financing long-term care. Incentives are now in place to encourage more people to purchase private LTC insurance.

One incentive offered by the federal government and some states comes in the form of tax advantages for the owners of certain types of policies. Before explaining these tax advantages, it's important to understand the difference between policies that have been granted guaranteed tax status and those that have not.

HIPAA DEFINES TAX-QUALIFIED LTC INSURANCE POLICIES

Prior to 1997, the lack of standardization in LTC insurance policies made them difficult for consumers to understand. While many consumers purchased coverage, an equal number of people avoided LTC insurance for two major reasons:

1. Their lack of understanding about long-term care in general
2. The confusing language in LTC insurance policies

Much of the confusing language was eliminated when the Health Insurance Portability and Accountability Act (HIPAA) became effective on January 1, 1997. This legislation produced long-needed standardization of LTC insurance policies and created tax-qualified (TQ) policies.

Passage of the HIPAA legislation also had many positive effects on other areas of the health insurance system. But many experts believe the most significant impact of the legislation was the "legitimization" of LTC insurance. Our legislators sent clear messages that (1) our government cannot afford to finance long-term care and (2) LTC insurance will play a major role in financing long-term care.

FAST FACTS:

■ The number of people receiving Social Security benefits between now and 2050 will increase by **100%**, while the number of workers will only increase by **22%**.

■ In 1940, there were 42 workers for every retiree; today, there are only 3 workers for every retiree. By 2050, this ratio is expected to be 2 to 1.

From a practical standpoint, TQ policies are written with easier-to-understand language, and other standardized consumer protections that are a part of every policy. At the time of claim, TQ policies offer a standardized set of criteria for determining eligibility for benefits.

Equally important is the standardized clarification of the tax advantages of TQ policies. HIPAA clarified that the benefits collected on TQ policies are guaranteed tax-free. The legislation also grants tax deductibility of premiums under certain conditions. Prior to HIPAA legislation, the tax ramifications of collecting on a policy were unclear and premiums were not tax deductible.

NON-TAX-QUALIFIED POLICIES

It's possible to purchase LTC insurance that is non-tax-qualified (NTQ). These policies do not meet HIPAA approval and are less standardized than TQ policies. The tax treatment of NTQ policies has not been firmly established.

Since HIPAA legislation was passed, there has been an ongoing debate in the LTC industry about the differences between NTQ and TQ long-term care insurance policies. Some mistakenly believe that NTQ policies are less restrictive at the time of claim. But in fact, NTQ policies may contain language that allows an insurance company too much discretion in determining eligibility for benefits.

Due to their standardization and tax qualifications, TQ policies are superior to NTQ policies, especially for *true* long-term care. In fact, most reputable insurance companies offer only TQ policies.

If you purchased an LTC insurance policy prior to January 1, 1997, when HIPAA legislation went into effect, your policy was "grandfathered into" tax-qualified status. This means that policies issued prior to passage of HIPAA contain protections with regard to the tax advantages, even though the legislation was not in force at the time the coverage was issued. This will remain true as long as you make no *material changes* to your "grandfathered" policy. An example of a *material change* would be submitting an application to the insurance carrier to increase the benefits of your existing policy.

CAUTION: Never replace or request a modification to an LTC insurance policy you purchased in the past without consulting your financial advisor and/or LTC Planning and Insurance expert *(for more information about replacing an existing policy, see Part 5: Questions and Answers)*.

The remainder of this section will explain the specific tax advantages of TQ long-term care insurance policies.

FEDERAL TAX ADVANTAGES TAKE THE FORM OF A TAX DEDUCTION

As of 2007, the federal government does not offer a tax *credit* to owners of LTC insurance. This has been seriously debated in Congress, and a tax credit is supported by respected organizations such as the American Medical Association. Most experts believe a federal tax credit will be granted in the future.

The federal government does offer tax advantages for owners of TQ long-term care insurance in the form of a tax *deduction*. Your filing status determines the rules for your federal income tax deduction.

Individuals (Non-Self-Employed) Use Form 1040 Schedule A

For individuals, premiums for LTC insurance may be deducted as a medical expense on your federal tax return, but only if you itemize on Form 1040 Schedule A. Your total amount of medical expenses added to the allowable amount of your LTC insurance premium *(see the Maximum Allowable Premium Deduction Chart)* must exceed 7.5% of your adjusted gross income. The amount in excess of 7.5% can then be deducted from your adjusted gross income.

Few individuals benefit from this tax break. A person spending as much as 7.5% of their adjusted gross income on medical expenses is not likely to be healthy enough to pass LTC insurance underwriting and be issued LTC insurance. However, if a policyholder's health declined after their policy was issued, and significant health care expenses were incurred, this deduction could become beneficial.

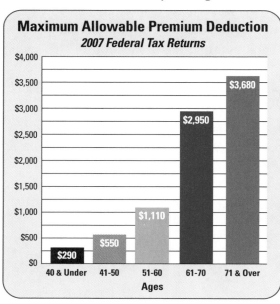

Maximum Allowable Premium Deduction
2007 Federal Tax Returns

Self-Employed Individuals, S-Corporations and LLCs

Self-employed individuals, S-Corporations, and LLCs have more meaningful tax advantages. These entities can deduct LTC insurance premiums for policies purchased for owners and others. For example, the company can deduct premiums paid for a spouse or other tax dependents, such as parents. If the parents are not dependents, the company may still have a tax deduction if the parents are employees of the company. A tax deduction can also be taken for premiums paid for any employees' relatives.

The deduction is taken as a health insurance premium expense, so the premium is deductible regardless of whether or not you itemize deductions. Premiums *are* subject to self-employment tax.

There are limits to the tax deduction for these business entities. The limit to the deduction is based on the age of the policyholder. The *Maximum Allowable Premium Deduction Chart* shows the age ranges and amount of deductible premium as of 2007. The IRS increases the allowable amount annually.

C-Corporations

C-Corporations enjoy the most favorable tax break. In fact, LTC insurance offered through C-Corporations can be beneficial from a tax standpoint for both the employer and the employee. The employer can create a substantial tax deduction for the company; and if the employee has a claim, the benefits paid from the policy are not counted as part of the employee's compensation.

C-Corporations can pay all or a portion of LTC insurance premiums for employees selected to receive the LTC insurance benefit. Employers who pay the premium for their employees are allowed to choose which employees receive the benefit: there is no requirement to purchase coverage for every employee.

The tax advantage to the employer is the deductibility of the **full amount** of the company's portion of the premium as a reasonable business expense. If the employee pays part or all of the premium, the employee is subject to the rules for "non-self-employed individuals" for their portion of the premium paid.

Caution: Anyone considering offering LTC insurance as a benefit to employees should first read *Chapter 17: Group and Sponsored Long-Term Care Insurance.*

No Section 125 "Cafeteria Plan" Status

Unfortunately, long-term care insurance **DOES NOT** qualify as a benefit under Section 125, "Cafeteria Plan" status. The result is that LTC insurance cannot be purchased with pre-tax dollars under an employer-provided benefits plan. This is a significant shortfall to offering LTC insurance as an employee benefit and explains why more employers do not offer coverage.

Using HSAs and MSAs to Pay LTC Insurance Premiums

Although LTC insurance premiums **cannot** be paid with funds in an IRA or 401K plan, premiums **can** be paid with funds in a Health Savings Account (HSA) or Medical Savings Account (MSA).

IRC Section 223(d)(2)(C) permits premiums for tax-qualified long-term care insurance policies to be considered as a qualified medical expense. This strategy **is** subject to the age based limits shown in the *"Maximum Allowable Premium Deduction"* chart.

See your financial professional and/or tax specialist for specific details and current rules regarding this tax strategy.

STATE TAX INCENTIVES FOR OWNING LTC INSURANCE

Many state governments are beginning to offer tax incentives to owners of TQ long-term care insurance policies. Unlike the federal government, some states **DO** offer a tax credit. Credits can be substantial because a tax credit directly reduces the amount of taxes you owe. When a state offers a tax credit to owners of LTC insurance, the tax credit is normally a percentage of the total premium paid.

Consult your financial professional or LTC Planning and Insurance expert for the current tax advantages offered in your state or, email us at: **info@superiorltc.com** for more information.

SEEK ADVICE FROM YOUR FINANCIAL PROFESSIONAL

Consult your financial professional and/or tax advisor for a complete explanation of the tax ramifications of LTC insurance for your specific situation.

KEY POINTS

Tax Advantages of Long-Term Care Insurance

➤ Lawmakers are concerned that Americans are not proactively planning ahead for long-term care. To alleviate part of this problem, certain LTC insurance policies offer tax advantages.

➤ HIPAA defined tax-qualified policies and standardized TQ long-term care insurance policies.

➤ Today's most reputable insurance companies offer only tax-qualified long-term care insurance policies.

➤ Policies purchased prior to January 1997 were granted tax-qualified status and will remain tax-qualified unless you make a *material change* to your policy.

➤ All federal tax advantages for long-term care insurance premiums are in the form of a tax deduction.

➤ Most states offer a tax deduction for long-term care insurance premiums; some offer a more powerful tax incentive: a tax credit.

Chapter 16 Partnership Policies

The significant problems we face
cannot be solved at the same level of
thinking we were at when we created them.

— Albert Einstein

In addition to tax incentives offered by states and the federal government, some states are offering serious incentives to plan ahead with LTC insurance. One program offers a promising solution to the huge challenge of providing long-term care to an increasing number of aging Americans. The program is known as the **"Partnership for Long-Term Care"** and uses a combination of public and private money to pay for care.

Currently, Partnership Programs are offered in California, Connecticut, Indiana, and New York. If you live in one of these states, ask your financial professional or LTC Planning and Insurance expert to offer advice about whether or not a Partnership policy is suitable for you. If LTC insurance is the option you are relying on for planning for long-term care, Partnership policies can be a good value.

HISTORY AND OBJECTIVES OF THE PARTNERSHIP PROGRAM

In 1986, the Robert Wood Johnson Foundation, a charitable organization instrumental in the development of the Partnership Program, issued grants to 10 states to fund the study of long-term care delivery and financing. The grants were also issued to assist states in developing solutions to the problem of funding long-term care for an increasing number of aging Americans.

The outcome of this research and assistance with developing solutions was the creation of the Partnership for Long-Term Care Program. The objectives of the Program include the following:

- Cap the amount of public monies used to finance long-term care.
- Improve consumers' understanding of the challenges of financing long-term care.
- Reduce consumers' fears of impoverishment due to a need for long-term care.
- Make LTC insurance more readily available to consumers.

Standardized Requirements of Each Partnership Policy

The Program requires standardized benefits that make the Partnership policies a unique consideration. Partnership policies must:

- Include inflation protection.
- Offer protection against unreasonable rate increases.
- Require agents offering the Partnership policies to be specifically trained and receive Partnership Certification.
- Include Care Coordination. This benefit may extend a policy's benefits and may assist the policyholder in locating providers of care *(see Chapter 14: Submitting a Claim)*.
- Allow claims to be made even if the policyholder moves from the state in which the policy was issued. However, in order to benefit from the "asset protection" component of the policy (explained below), the claimant would need to move back to the issuing state. The exception is Indiana and Connecticut: in 2001, these two states approved a reciprocity agreement.
- Protect you if your state decides to discontinue the Partnership Program: your policy remains contractually protected as long as premiums are paid.

PARTNERSHIP COMPANIES ARE SUPERIOR

The Partnership Program policies are private LTC insurance, underwritten by a select few, high-quality insurance companies. Partnership Program insurance companies must go through a stringent approval process in order to offer Partnership policies. A company willing to become approved to offer Partnership policies is making a major commitment to the LTC insurance industry. This commitment makes companies offering Partnership policies superior to other LTC insurance companies.

HOW DOES THE PARTNERSHIP PROGRAM WORK?

Partnership policies contain an **"asset protection"** component that allows people to shelter some or all of their assets by linking the purchase of private LTC insurance with future eligibility for Medicaid, the welfare program (Medi-Cal in California). A policyholder first uses their Partnership policy benefits to pay for long-term care expenses. If and when the benefits of the policy are exhausted, the policyholder will become eligible for Medicaid, without being required to first spend all their assets on care. This allows a person who owns an LTC insurance policy certified through the Partnership Program to qualify for Medicaid without having to follow the usual "spend-down" rules that impoverish most families. (Some of these Medicaid rules are explained in *Chapter 4.*) The Partnership Program essentially allows you to keep some or all of your assets, without being required to totally deplete your money paying for long-term care.

The Programs in California, Connecticut, and Indiana are based on a **dollar-for-dollar** model of coverage: for every dollar of LTC insurance coverage that you purchase under the Partnership Program, a dollar of your assets is protected from the spend-down requirements for Medicaid eligibility. Connecticut offers a "bonus:" facilities in that state must offer Partnership policyholders a 5% discount off their published daily room rates.

Example of How a Partnership Policy Works

If a policyholder wants to protect $500,000 in non-exempt assets, he or she could purchase a Partnership policy with a maximum lifetime benefit of $500,000. When the policyholder becomes eligible for benefits, the insurer will pay for long-term care expenses up to $500,000, plus any inflation-adjusted benefits that have increased the coverage due to the inflation protection benefit of the policy. After the total maximum lifetime benefit is paid out by the insurance company, the policyholder could then be eligible for Medicaid benefits, but maintain assets up to the total dollar benefit paid by the policy.

The New York Partnership Program differs in that it's based on the **total-assets protection** model. Partnership Certified policies must cover at least three years in a facility or six years of home care, with minimum daily benefit amounts that are raised annually. Once the Partnership policy benefits are exhausted, the Medicaid eligibility process will allow the policyholder to keep an unlimited amount of assets. However, an individual's income must contribute to the cost of care. The New York Partnership formally states that "the goal of the Partnership is to help people finance long-term care without impoverishing themselves or losing their life savings. At the same time, the program will help to reduce New York's massive Medicaid expenditures."

The Partnership Program is a true "Partnership" between the policyholder and the government because it allows participants to keep some or all of their assets, *if* they purchase a Partnership LTC insurance policy and use their insurance benefits prior to applying for assistance from Medicaid.

FUTURE OF THE PARTNERSHIP PROGRAM

The success of the Partnership Program in the original states has encouraged other states to seek waivers so that they can offer Partnership Programs in their state. In fact, Congress passed the Deficit Reduction Act in 2006, which is already expanding the availability of Partnership Programs to other states. If you do not live in one of the original Partnership states, ask your financial professional and LTC Planning and Insurance expert if a Partnership Program has become available in your state since the publication of this information.

An insightful history and philosophical overview of the Partnership Program is in *Chapter 19,* where we interview Dr. James Knickman, a leader in the development of the Partnership Program, and Vice-President of Research and Evaluation at the Robert Wood Johnson Foundation.

KEY POINTS

Partnership Programs

➤ Partnership Programs use a combination of private and public dollars to pay for long-term care.

➤ Under a Partnership Program, policyholders can keep some or all of their assets and still qualify for Medicaid. Long-term care insurance is used first to pay for long-term care expenses. When the policy benefits are exhausted, the policyholder may become eligible for Medicaid without having to spend down all their assets.

➤ Insurance companies that offer Partnership policies are superior to insurance companies that do not.

➤ Most experts believe that programs such as the Partnership Program offer the most promising solution to financing the long-term care crisis.

➤ The Deficit Reduction Act was passed in 2006 and made it possible for Partnership policies to become available in most states.

Chapter 17 **Group and Sponsored Long-Term Care Insurance**

Success is practically guaranteed with one simple step:
Carefully observe the group and do exactly the opposite.

— Earl Nightingale, *Author*

Many employers are searching for ways to help their employees avoid becoming primary caregivers in the future. In a study conducted by LifePlans, Inc, it was learned that LTC insurance benefits clearly reduce the caregiver workload for employees caring for loved ones. Some employers believe that offering LTC insurance as an incentive will attract and retain quality employees.

LTC insurance can also be offered through an association, financial institution, or other group. Prior to considering coverage offered through your workplace, association, bank, or any other type of group or sponsored promotion, read this chapter and ask for advice from your financial professional.

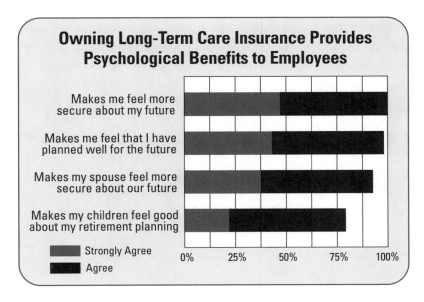

FAST FACTS:

■ Long-term care insurance **DOES NOT** qualify as a benefit under Section 125, "Cafeteria Plan" status. This means that coverage cannot be purchased with pre-tax dollars under an employer-provided benefits plan.

■ Individually issued LTC insurance is normally a better value than group and sponsored LTC insurance.

Some agents and insurance companies promote the myth that group and sponsored coverage is a good value in the majority of situations. Although there are some people who can benefit from a group or sponsored offering, LTC insurance offered with this approach should never be *automatically* purchased. As you will learn in the "Advantages" and "Disadvantages" sections of this chapter, you will almost always receive a better value by purchasing individually issued LTC insurance.

SIGNIFICANT SHORTFALL FOR EMPLOYERS AND EMPLOYEES

In *Chapter 15,* we explained that there can be tax advantages for employers who offer LTC insurance as an employee benefit. For example, C-Corporations may deduct 100% of the premium, while the benefits paid on a claim are not subject to taxation.

We also explained that long-term care insurance **DOES NOT** qualify as a benefit under Section 125, "Cafeteria Plan" status. This means that coverage cannot be purchased with pre-tax dollars under an employer-provided benefits plan. This is a significant shortfall to offering LTC insurance as an employee benefit and explains why more employers do not offer coverage.

LONG-TERM CARE INSURANCE THROUGH YOUR WORKPLACE

Long-term care insurance could be offered through your workplace with either a "true" group program or a "sponsored" program.

Group Long-Term Care Insurance

Many of the basic factors that affect the premium of individually issued LTC insurance *(explained in Chapter 10)* are also true with group LTC insurance. However, group LTC insurance has some distinct disadvantages to individually issued coverage.

Disadvantages of Group LTC Insurance:

1. The group market is championed by traditional insurance agents utilizing a *single sales approach.* LTC Planning should always be integrated with your financial and estate plan. Your financial advisor, not an insurance agent, is in the best position to give you initial guidance in planning for long-term care. After giving you initial guidance, your financial advisor should refer you to an LTC Planning expert certified in the *Comprehensive Planning Approach* to long-term care.

2. Group coverage normally uses a "cookie-cutter" approach to coverage: In order to assist agents in making sales, insurance companies usually narrow the benefit choices to a few simple options. This makes it difficult to obtain customized coverage that addresses your unique situation.

3. Unlike most types of group insurance coverage, group LTC insurance is normally **more** expensive, not less expensive, than individually issued coverage (when comparing identical benefits). For healthy people, an individually issued policy results in a better value than a group issued LTC insurance policy.

   Group coverage is more expensive because of a problem called **Adverse Selection:** group coverage allows the issuance of LTC insurance to individuals who would not normally pass typical underwriting requirements. LTC insurance sold through a group policy is normally issued with health underwriting standards that are not as strict as individually issued coverage. This results in coverage being issued to many people who are already in poor health.

   Group LTC insurance is usually offered on either a **Guaranteed Issue** basis, or a **Modified Guaranteed Issue** basis. Guaranteed Issue offers any employee, regardless of health, the right to obtain coverage, without being required to pass any underwriting requirements. Modified Guaranteed Issue means that people in extremely poor health may not qualify. But as long as a person can certify that they are not currently needing long-term care services, or as long as they have not been diagnosed with a major health condition that will require long-term care in the near future, they will likely qualify for coverage under a Modified Guaranteed Issue program.

Adverse Selection results in a substantially higher than average number of claims than claims submitted by policyholders who were issued coverage with stringent underwriting requirements. Because claims are higher, healthy people who purchase coverage through the group subsidize the current premiums as well as premium increases caused by the claims of people in poor health. As a result, group LTC insurance is usually more expensive initially than individual policies, and will experience higher and more frequent rate increases in the future.

Adverse Selection is made worse because group LTC insurance is usually offered on a voluntary basis. The offering will be attractive to individuals who are already in poor health and know they can't obtain coverage on an individual basis. A study conducted in 2001 among buyers of group LTC insurance proved this by revealing that the number one reason for purchasing group coverage was the employee's belief that they face a much greater-than-average risk of needing care. This is not good news for healthy people who participate in a group offering.

> ## *If you are in good health, avoid group LTC insurance because:*
>
> - You are subsidizing a higher premium for those who are not healthy.
> - The poor health of many participants increases the odds of higher premium rates in the future.
> - Your LTC insurance plan design will be more customized using the *Comprehensive Planning Approach*. The insurance agent offering the group program will likely use a *single sales approach*.

One Advantage of Group LTC Insurance:

There is one situation where group LTC insurance is worth considering: If your financial professional has recommended LTC insurance, but your health is not good enough to qualify for individually issued coverage, you may want to consider any group coverage that may be available to you. If you decide the group coverage is appropriate, ask your advisor to refer you to an LTC Planning and Insurance expert for assistance in selecting the most appropriate benefits within the "cookie cutter" group policy options being offered. This will result in coverage that is as close as possible to a customized solution.

When evaluating the coverage offered by the group, request information about the financial rating of the insurance company issuing the coverage. As explained in *Chapter 12,* it's imperative to have coverage with a company rated **A** or higher with A.M. Best. An insurance company with a rating lower than **A** that offers a Guaranteed Issue or Modified Guaranteed Issue group LTC insurance policy has higher odds of experiencing financial problems. This could compromise your ability to collect policy benefits after paying the premiums for a number of years. Almost as detrimental, such carriers are likely to impose such frequent and substantial rate increases that the coverage becomes unaffordable.

Sponsored Long-Term Care Insurance

Sponsored LTC insurance programs may be offered by your employer; financial institution such as a credit union, bank or stock brokerage firm; Chamber of Commerce; professional association; senior or retirement association such as AARP; or some other group. Insurance companies offer sponsored LTC insurance policies that are marketed by agents, or through marketing campaigns, such as advertisements, direct mail, phone solicitations, or by internet and email.

Sponsored LTC insurance is a better value for healthy people than group LTC insurance policies. Since they use the same stringent underwriting guidelines as individually issued policies, sponsored programs are not likely to experience the adverse selection problems of group LTC insurance programs. But sponsored offerings almost always fail to offer the best overall value.

Disadvantages of Sponsored LTC Insurance:

1. There is only one insurance company sponsoring the program, so you're limited to the narrow coverage options offered by the one company. A plan offered by another carrier may give you more appropriate coverage options for your unique situation.

2. Some sponsored programs may advertise a 5%-10% discount, but the discounted premium could be a marketing gimmick. In reality, the discounted premium may be higher than the normal premium rate with an alternative insurance company. Ask your LTC Planning and Insurance expert for premium comparisons and benefits among several top-rated insurance carriers, prior to considering any sponsored offering.

3. As with group coverage, sponsored offerings are sometimes promoted by insurance agents who sell LTC insurance using the *single sales approach* rather than utilizing the *Comprehensive Planning Approach.*

4. If an agent is not involved, the insurance company is selling coverage directly, either over the phone, by internet, or through the mail. Buying directly from the carrier saves no money, and leaves you to deal directly with the company at the time of claim, instead of having an unbiased service representative to assist you with your claim.

One Advantage of Sponsored LTC Insurance:

There is one situation where sponsored LTC insurance is worth considering: When the employer, association, or other organization uses the services of an LTC Planning and Insurance expert certified in the *Comprehensive Planning Approach* to long-term care. In this situation, you may get the best of all worlds:

- The ability to choose coverage among several top-rated insurance carriers.

- The advantage of having your LTC plan and policy design integrated with your personal and financial objectives.

- The possibility of receiving a 5%-10% discount on the premium.

Organizations Considering a Program Should Use Caution

If your employer, financial institution, professional or retirement association, or group of any kind is considering a sponsored program, the LTC Planning and Insurance expert chosen to administer the program directly affects the reputation of your company or organization. Decision makers in your organization should get thorough answers to the questions below when interviewing potential LTC Planning and Insurance professionals. For a complete list of questions to ask, email us at **interviewchecklist@superiorltc.com**.

INTERVIEWING POTENTIAL LTC PLANNING AND INSURANCE PROFESSIONALS

Questions about How Insurance Companies are Selected

- What criteria do you use to choose the insurance companies you recommend?

- How can we be sure the companies are reasonable in their underwriting and premium rates?

- What are the odds that the insurance companies you recommend will remain in the LTC insurance market?

Questions about Service

- What is the claim's payment history of the insurance companies you recommend?

- Will you provide our (members, customers, or employees) with assistance at the time of claim?

- Can you provide us with the names and phone numbers of others who have received assistance with their claims?

Questions about Future Service

- Who will service our (members, customers, or employees) if you personally retire or otherwise leave your profession?

- What selection criteria will be used if you are replaced with another representative?

GROUP AND SPONSORED PROGRAMS

	ADVANTAGES	DISADVANTAGES
GROUP	Guaranteed/Modified Issue coverage may allow people in poor health to obtain long-term care insurance when they would otherwise not qualify for an individually issued policy	Long-term care insurance sold with the *single sales approach*. Coverage is not normally integrated with your personal and financial objectives **Adverse Selection** allows those in poor health to obtain coverage, resulting in higher initial premiums for those in good health. This also raises the risk of increasingly higher premium rates in the future Limited to the coverage options offered by the one insurance company offering the coverage. This eliminates the opportunity to compare coverage and premium rates among various carriers
SPONSORED	Possible discount of 5%–10% Working with an LTC Planning and Insurance expert certified in the *Comprehensive Planning Approach* may offer additional advantages: • Choice of multiple top-rated carriers • LTC plan and policy design developed within the context of your personal and financial objectives • Assistance at time of claim	Long-term care insurance sold with the *single sales approach*. Coverage is not normally integrated with your personal and financial objectives Even with a discount, premium may be higher than coverage offered by an alternative carrier Limited to the coverage options offered by the one insurance company offering the coverage. This eliminates the opportunity to compare coverage and premium rates among various carriers

KEY POINTS

Group and Sponsored Long-Term Care Insurance

➤ Group long-term care insurance is typically issued with lenient underwriting standards, causing healthy policyholders to subsidize the premium of people in poor health.

➤ Group plans attract people who are already in poor health and cannot obtain long-term care insurance any other way.

➤ **Adverse Selection** results when the group of policyholders includes more people in poor health and fewer in excellent health. As a result, the insurance company has a higher-than-average number of claims and charges higher premium rates, with high odds of increasingly higher premium rates in the future.

➤ Sponsored long-term care insurance policies are offered through employers, retirement associations, financial institutions, and other groups.

➤ Sponsored policies are superior to true group policies because they are individually issued, and use a stringent underwriting process. But sponsored programs normally fail to offer the best overall value. The exception is a sponsored program that enlists the services of an LTC Planning and Insurance expert certified in the *Comprehensive Planning Approach* to long-term care.

PART

5

Questions & Answers about Long-Term Care Insurance

*Never let your schoolin' get
in the way of your education.*

— Mark Twain

PART 5:
Questions & Answers about Long-Term Care Insurance

Over the years, we have been asked thousands of questions about long-term care insurance. We've answered the majority of those questions in the previous pages. But some questions were difficult to incorporate into the general text. These miscellaneous questions will be answered in this section. If you have a specific question that is not addressed here or in the general text, ask your financial advisor or email your question to: **info@superiorltc.com**.

GENERAL QUESTIONS ABOUT LTC INSURANCE

Q. A financial advisor on television continuously states that LTC insurance should only be considered by people over a certain age. This advisor has used two ages as "ideal" for purchasing coverage: age 54 and age 59. Is she right?

A. No. This subject is discussed in several areas of this book, and specifically in *Chapters 9 and 18*. This erroneous advice is the most prevalent and dangerous myth in LTC Planning.

Whether or not to purchase LTC insurance has nothing to do with your age. It has to do with whether or not you have prioritized your insurance needs, whether or not you can afford the LTC insurance premium, your tolerance for risk, and other factors.

There are a number of reasons why "blanket advice" to wait until a "perfect age" before considering LTC insurance is dangerous to both consumers and to financial advisors giving such advice:

1. Long-term care insurance premiums rise with each year a person waits to purchase coverage and are also on the rise in the industry in general.

2. While waiting until the "perfect age" to purchase coverage, many consumers will become uninsurable, and some may even begin needing long-term care.

3. Financial advisors who give this advice may find themselves involved in litigation with consumers or their clients (and/or their heirs) who heeded this advice, and later find they can no longer afford coverage, or no longer qualify for coverage. This is particularly true if the person later needs long-term care.

Q. *Is there an age at which LTC insurance becomes unattainable?*

A. Some insurance companies issue coverage to age 84. However, most carriers restrict the benefit choices for applicants over age 79. This means that even if the applicant qualifies for coverage, the benefit options may be very narrow. LTC insurance is rarely issued at older ages, due to the likelihood of poor health and unaffordable premiums.

Q. *Are policies that combine life insurance and LTC insurance a good value?*

A. No. These insurance policies are referred to by different names, including "Combination Policies," "Bundled Policies," or "Accelerated Death Benefit Policies."

The policy is usually a life insurance policy with an LTC insurance rider that can be used to pay for long-term care expenses. In other words, instead of having to die to receive benefits, the policy could pay benefits to cover the cost of the policyholder's long-term care expenses.

These policies are sold as a "gimmick," to people who refuse to pay for insurance coverage they may never use. The sales pitch emphasizes that the policyholder can own insurance coverage, and always be assured that a benefit will be paid. The agent tells the prospective buyer: "If long-term care is not needed, at least your beneficiary will receive benefits from the life insurance portion of the policy."

The sales pitch is enticing and the agent can make it seem so simple. But don't be fooled into believing you are getting something for free—insurance companies do not "give away" insurance. With this type of policy, you are actually paying for two types of insurance coverage, whether you need both types or not: life insurance and long-term care insurance. If you use the long-term care portion of the coverage, the life insurance coverage is reduced proportionately.

For example, if you bought a $100,000 life insurance policy with an LTC insurance rider, and then collected $75,000 for long-term care expenses, your beneficiary would collect only $25,000 at your death. But you've paid a premium for $100,000 in life insurance benefits, as well as a premium for the long-term care insurance benefit.

Ask your financial professional to advise you on each of your insurance needs separately. If life insurance is appropriate, purchase the best life insurance value for your particular situation. Do not bundle the coverage with another type of insurance. If life insurance is not appropriate, then don't purchase it at all.

The same is true with LTC insurance. Ask your financial professional to advise you on your options. If LTC insurance is appropriate, purchase the best LTC insurance value for your particular situation. Do not bundle the coverage with another type of insurance. If LTC insurance is not appropriate, don't purchase it at all.

Q. Can a person who would qualify for Medicaid, the welfare program, purchase LTC insurance?

A. No. People who qualify for Medicaid do not need LTC insurance because the welfare system will pay for their care. In fact, it is illegal for an insurance agent to solicit, or an insurance company to issue an LTC insurance policy, to an individual who qualifies for Medicaid benefits. Every LTC insurance application includes a specific question about whether or not an applicant is Medicaid-eligible.

Q. What is the difference between Guaranteed Renewable and Non-Cancelable LTC insurance?

A. Guaranteed Renewable policies guarantee that the policy must be renewed for life, as long as premium payments are paid on time. However, the insurance company reserves the right to increase the premium—as long as the premium increase is implemented on a class basis—not an individual basis.

Non-cancelable policies guarantee that (1) the policy is renewable for life if premium payments are paid on time, and (2) the insurance company can never increase the premium rates, even on a class basis.

Although insurance companies have offered non-cancelable policies in the past, there are none available at the time of this writing. You may, however, purchase a rider that guarantees your premium rate will not be increased for a specified number of years. But the best strategy for avoiding frequent rate increases is to follow the advice given in *Chapter 12: Choosing the Right Insurance Carrier.*

Q. *Can a person purchase an LTC insurance policy for a parent or someone else, without them knowing that the coverage has been purchased?*

A. No. The person who will be insured must consent to the coverage by signing an application. They must also be fully aware of the purpose of the application, understand the policy benefits, and understand the underwriting process.

However, a person may pay the premium for another person. In many cases, children pay the premium for their parents' LTC insurance coverage. *(This is explained in more detail in Chapter 8: Why People Choose Long-Term Care Insurance as Their Plan.)*

Q. *If a person already owns an LTC insurance policy, should they ever replace the policy?*

A. The decision of whether or not to replace a current policy should be taken very seriously and analyzed by your financial advisor and LTC Planning and Insurance expert. In most cases, you have more to lose than gain by replacing an existing policy. But each situation is unique, and should be analyzed by considering the following questions:

- Is your current insurance carrier financially stable and committed to the LTC insurance industry? Do they increase your premium rates frequently?

- Has your health changed for the worse since you purchased the policy? If so, you may not qualify if you applied for coverage today.

- How long ago was the policy purchased? A policy purchased several years ago probably has a fairly low premium compared to the premium of newly issued coverage today. This may be true even if your current carrier has increased your premium rate.

Q. Is it important to work with an LTC Planning and Insurance expert who can offer coverage with multiple carriers?

A. It's absolutely essential. We recommend that you never purchase LTC insurance from an agent or financial advisor who represents only one company. An agent or advisor who only represents one company has a very strong allegiance to that company. They will have difficulty being unbiased and may act more on behalf of the insurance company than you at claim's time.

You should trust **one** independent LTC Planning and Insurance expert specifically certified in the *Comprehensive Planning Approach.* This person should be referred to you by your financial planner, estate planning attorney, or CPA. They should be licensed with several top-rated insurance carriers. This allows you to see benefit comparisons from a number of carriers without spending time with several different advisors.

Q. Is there a safety net in place for policyholders who have coverage with an insurance company that becomes insolvent?

A. *Chapter 12* explains the importance of carefully choosing an insurance carrier. By following the guidelines explained in that chapter, your chances of having to face this issue are greatly reduced.

But there are protections in place if the company insuring you becomes insolvent. Most states operate "Guaranty Funds." These programs are designed to become the insurer for policyholders who have purchased coverage from carriers that become insolvent. The specific benefits of Guaranty Funds and the way they operate vary from state to state. Ask your financial advisor or contact your state's insurance department for more specifics about the availability of a Guaranty Fund in your state.

Q. What happens if I buy an LTC insurance policy, and the insurance company later decides to stop offering LTC insurance to future applicants?

A. All individually issued policies sold today are guaranteed renewable. This means that the company cannot cancel your policy as long as you pay your premium on time. This is true even if the company decides to no longer offer coverage to future applicants.

Policies issued in earlier years and group coverage may or may not be "guaranteed renewable," and thus may be cancelable. If you currently own an LTC insurance policy, look for the words **"Guaranteed Renewable"** on the front of the policy. Other terminology such as "Portable" and "Entitled to continue after retirement or divorce" are ***NOT*** sufficient substitutes for the term "Guaranteed Renewable". If your policy is not guaranteed renewable, you may want to consider replacing the policy. As with our recommendation throughout this book, seek the advice of your financial advisor prior to canceling, replacing, or making any modifications whatsoever to a currently in-force LTC insurance policy. *(For more on the implications of insurance companies exiting the long-term care insurance market, see the Introduction to Part 3.)*

Q. What recourse does a policyholder have if they believe they have a legitimate complaint to file against an insurer or an agent?

A. Your best defense against a problem with an insurance company or an insurance agent is to follow our advice in *Chapter 12* about carefully choosing an insurance carrier, and our advice about working with an expert who is certified in the *Comprehensive Planning Approach*.

But if you purchased coverage from someone you believe has not served you ethically, or from an insurance company that you believe has not treated you fairly, contact the Insurance Department in your state. Each state's insurance department has a formal process for filing a complaint.

*Q. **Is there an insurance policy that covers "Short-Term Care?"***

A. Yes. Short-term care insurance policies cover you for less than one year of care. In order for a policy to be called "long-term care insurance," the maximum lifetime benefit must be at least one year.

Short-term care insurance is not a good value. These policies are designed for people who can't afford LTC insurance. It's unlikely that people who can't afford LTC insurance will receive much benefit from a short-term care policy. These policies are mainly designed to help insurance agents make sales to consumers who were initially interested in LTC insurance, but found the premium to be too high.

*Q. **What is your opinion of the Federal LTC Insurance Program (FLTCIP)?***

A. When a new law went into effect in 2002 creating the Federal LTC Insurance Program, the federal government sent a clear signal that long-term care financing through government entitlement programs will be limited in the future.

FLTCIP is a long-term care insurance program available to federal employees, including military personnel. The program is not a guaranteed issue program—underwriting takes place with each application.

We recommend that a person who qualifies for this program ask their financial advisor for a referral to an LTC Planning and Insurance expert to assist them in determining whether or not this program is a good value for their situation. In particular, it's important to thoroughly understand the implications of the "Catastrophic Coverage Limitation" clause contained in this coverage, which could limit the maximum benefits of the coverage. In most cases, a better value can be obtained by avoiding the FLTCIP coverage and obtaining an individually issued policy.

QUESTIONS ABOUT LTC INSURANCE PREMIUMS

Q. What is a "Limited-Pay" LTC insurance policy?

A. A Limited-Pay policy allows you to "pay-up" your LTC insurance coverage in a certain pre-determined number of years. This means that instead of paying your LTC insurance premiums for the rest of your life, you limit the number of years of payments.

Payment options for limited-pay policies are:

• Single Pay: one large premium payment

• Pay for 5 years

• Pay for 10 years

• Pay for 20 years

• Pay until age 65

There are advantages and disadvantages to choosing a limited-pay policy:

Advantages:

1. Maybe your goal is to retire in 10 years, and you would rather not make premium payments during your retirement years. Paying for coverage during your income-earning years allows you to have coverage with no out-of-pocket premium payments once the coverage is paid-up.

2. If the insurance company has a rate increase after your policy is paid-up, the company cannot ask you to pay additional premium. Once these policies are paid in full, they remain so for life.

3. If you purchase the inflation-protection rider, the benefits of the policy continue to increase, even after the policy is paid-up. Your benefits continue to increase in value even though you are no longer making premium payments.

Disadvantages:

1. The premium for limited-pay policies is higher than premiums for "pay-for-life" policies. For example, the premium for a "pay-for-10-years" policy is generally between 2 and 3 times higher than a "pay-for-life" policy.

2. If you are not able to keep your LTC insurance policy in force because, for example, your finances change and you can no longer afford the premium, purchasing a limited pay policy would be a more costly financial mistake.

3. If you go on permanent claim during the premium payment years and the policy is placed on waiver of premium (see Glossary), you have paid extra premium for no gain in extra benefit.

Limited-pay policies can be a good choice for business owners who plan to retire in a pre-determined number of years. In addition, they may benefit from tax advantages, by deducting the premium as a business expense. *(This is explained in more detail in Chapter 15: Tax Advantages of Long-Term Care Insurance.)* High-income-earning executives, who may be in their last 5 to 20 years of employment are also good candidates for considering limited-pay policies.

Q. *Are there ways to obtain discounts on LTC insurance premiums?*

A. Yes. You can obtain several types of discounts with the same policy. For example, most companies offer a spousal or partner discount. This discount is negligible with some companies and substantial with others. A discount of 10% to 20% is typical.

Another discount can be obtained by those in excellent health. This discount averages 15% with most companies.

But whether or not the company offers a discount, and the discount percentage, is less important than comparing coverage and premium rates among several top-rated insurance companies. One company may offer substantial discounts on a percentage basis, but the overall premium will be higher than the premium on a policy offered by an insurance company that offers lower percentage discounts.

*Q. **Do LTC insurance policies offer a grace period for paying the premium?***

A. By law, individually issued LTC insurance policies have a grace period of at least 31 days: the insured has up to 31 days after the due date to make sure the premium is received by the insurance company. After that period, the insurance company can terminate the policy.

*Q. **Is it true that premium rates on issued policies can never be raised?***

A. Unfortunately, this is **not** true but is a common misconception. While premium rates cannot be raised due to advancing age, deteriorating health, or claims, the carrier **can** apply for a "class-wide" rate increase, which will affect all policyholders who have the same policy "form" from that particular company. You can reduce your chances of having frequent premium rate increases by following the guidelines offered in *Chapter 12: Choosing the Right Insurance Carrier.*

*Q. **If an insurance company has a premium rate increase on an LTC insurance policy, does the policyholder have options other than to pay the higher premium?***

A. Yes. If a rate increase is issued, the insurance company must offer the policyholder the option of reducing the policy benefits instead of paying the rate increase. This allows the policyholder to maintain the same premium rate but with reduced policy benefits.

QUESTIONS ABOUT LTC INSURANCE BENEFITS

Q. *What is the "Reduced Home Care" and "Reduced Assisted Living Facility" benefit, which is available with some Comprehensive LTC Insurance Policies?*

A. Comprehensive LTC Insurance Policies pay for care in any environment: your home, an assisted living community, or a nursing home. As explained in *Chapter 10,* we recommend Comprehensive LTC Insurance as opposed to coverage that only pays for care in one environment.

Some Comprehensive LTC Insurance Policies allow you to purchase a benefit amount for home care or assisted living facility care that is less than the benefit amount you purchase for nursing home care. For example, if you elect a daily benefit amount for nursing home care of $150 per day, you may be able to choose a reduced home care or assisted living facility care benefit amount of half that amount, or $75 per day. Choosing the reduced benefit will save an insignificant amount on the overall premium.

We **do not** recommend choosing the reduced benefit option. Choosing this option may force you into a nursing home due to the low coverage amount for benefits to stay at home or receive care in an assisted living facility.

Q. *What is the "Caregiver Training" benefit of an LTC insurance policy?*

A. When a policyholder needs long-term care services, the family may want to hire someone they personally trust to assist in caring for the loved one. The "Caregiver Training" benefit pays for specific training that may be needed to assist the policyholder. For example, training may be provided to teach skills needed to care for a patient with Alzheimer's Disease. Or, training could be provided to teach a person to use special equipment or administer medications. This benefit is included in most Comprehensive LTC Insurance Policies.

Q. *What is the "Bed Reservation" benefit of an LTC insurance policy?*

A. There are times when residents of assisted living communities or nursing homes need to be hospitalized for short periods of time. When this happens, there's a chance that the resident could lose their room at the facility because the facility is not obligated to "save" the patient's room unless the patient pays the fee during their absence. In response to this situation, the LTC insurance industry designed the "bed reservation" benefit, which is included in most Comprehensive LTC Insurance Policies. The benefit states that the insurance company will continue to pay for the room in the facility during the temporary absence of the policyholder. The bed reservation benefit varies by policy, but usually pays benefits for 15 to 30 days per year.

Q. *If a person has minor health conditions, but is issued long-term care coverage, will the insurance company pay a claim caused by one of the existing health conditions if the claim occurs immediately after the policy is issued? In other words, are there pre-existing condition clauses in LTC insurance policies?*

A. No, there are no pre-existing condition clauses. Therefore, the policy will pay benefits if a legitimate claim is submitted immediately after the policy is issued, even if the claim is the result of an existing health condition. However, you must disclose any health condition(s) at the time of application. A misrepresentation on your application could cause a claim to be denied. *It's important to answer all medical questions on the application correctly and thoroughly.*

PART 6

Financial Professionals: Assuring Your Clients' Choice, Independence and Financial Security

When planning for a year,
plant corn.

When planning for a decade,
plant trees.

When planning for life,
train and educate people.

— Chinese Proverb

PART 6:

Financial Professionals: Assuring Your Clients' Choice, Independence and Financial Security

Financial professionals, including financial planners, estate planning attorneys, and CPAs, are in the best position to assist clients with initiating the development of a written plan for long-term care. You understand your clients' financial situations, their goals, and their philosophies regarding risk management. You are the one they trust for advice and guidance concerning money matters of all kinds, particularly those that have a potentially detrimental effect on their family's financial security. LTC Planning is an essential area of service for financial professionals because you are entrusted with protecting the assets and estates of your clients.

THE OBLIGATIONS OF A FINANCIAL PROFESSIONAL

If financial professionals fail to address a financial risk with their clients, can they be held liable for such an omission? What if a client presumes that his or her estate and/or financial plan is secure and complete and then a long-term care event depletes or totally drains his or her financial portfolio? Would this be a legitimate case for filing a charge of malpractice?

Two respected journals have published information that signals a potential risk to financial professionals:

- The *Elder Law Journal* (Hayes 1999) published:
  Attorneys who advise clients about future financial security and concerns fulfill their professional obligation when they provide informed counsel in the area of long-term care...if (attorneys) are not informed about the nuances of long-term care insurance, they may be held liable if a client sues them for negligence.

- The *Journal of Financial Planning* (2001) published:
  Harley Gordon, Attorney at Law, identifies two specific areas of concern for financial professionals, including financial planners, estate planning attorneys, and CPAs:

1. The financial professional's failure to include the need to have a long-term care plan in his/her overall financial planning, estate planning, and/or retirement planning process.

2. Failure to address the need for LTC Planning with **wealthy** clients. Without guidance from a financial professional, wealthy people may presume they should automatically rely on their own assets to pay for the high costs of long-term care.

The warning signs point to the need for financial professionals to raise their clients' awareness of the significant financial impact of long-term care—a risk that has already negatively affected the financial security of thousands of families.

FINANCIAL PLANNERS

Financial planners fulfill their professional roles by advising their clients on a variety of financial topics.

LTC Planning is an integral component of the financial planning process, and a specific part of the risk management category of financial planning. *(This is explained in Chapter 6: Integrating Long-Term Care Planning with Financial & Estate Planning.)*

ESTATE PLANNING ATTORNEYS

As America's population continues to age, the need to integrate LTC Planning into an estate plan cannot be overlooked. Ignoring this crucial area can result in loss of inheritance, repayment of long-term care costs to the government through Estate Recovery programs, and other negative estate transfer consequences.

Therefore, estate planning attorneys are becoming more aware of the need to initiate LTC Planning with their clients. The Estate Planning and LTC Planning disciplines have the same objectives:

• Protection of Assets
• Preservation of Legacy

CPAs

Many CPAs are expanding their practice from exclusively being tax experts to including comprehensive financial and estate planning as part of the services they provide. In this role, CPAs are offering some of the additional services outlined in *Chapter 6.*

Regarding the individual and corporate tax ramifications of LTC Planning and LTC insurance, CPAs are in the best position to offer guidance and advice. *(See Chapter 15: Tax Advantages of Long-Term Care Insurance.)*

Many business owners are also asking their CPA about the feasibility of offering LTC insurance as an employee benefit. *(See Chapter 17: Group and Sponsored Long-Term Care Insurance.)*

YOUR CHALLENGE

A major roadblock for financial professionals who know they need to assist their clients with LTC Planning has been the availability of resources for competently addressing this issue. This book provides a foundation for understanding this subject, along with the basic education you need to initiate a discussion about LTC Planning with your clients and to offer them initial guidance.

We have also developed additional processes to assist with LTC Planning for your clients. The end result for each client is a permanently archived written plan for long-term care. Contact us at **www.superiorltc.com** to learn more about how we can assist you and your clients with LTC Planning.

Chapter 18 **LTC Planning and Insurance Myths**
by Steve Bell, CFP®

The great enemy of the truth is very often not the lie—deliberate, contrived, and dishonest— but the myth—persistent, persuasive, and realistic.
— John F. Kennedy

Many financial professionals avoid the issue of LTC Planning because of long-held myths regarding which clients are good candidates for planning ahead. The two most prevalent myths pertain to the "best" age for a person to begin planning (most financial professionals believe younger clients should wait), and a person's net worth (some professionals set an upper-end dollar figure at which people should automatically rely on their own assets).

This chapter addresses a few of the commonly held myths about age and net worth, and highlights the importance of educating *every* client about LTC Planning. *(To simplify this discussion, we will use the term "financial professional" to define a financial planner, estate planning attorney, or CPA.)*

SIX MYTHS THAT COULD RUIN YOUR CLIENTS' FINANCIAL FUTURE... AND YOURS

Clients rely on you, their trusted financial professional, to address any major risks to their financial and estate plans, and to recommend appropriate preventative measures. This is especially true in areas such as death, disability, fire, theft, accident, and liability. But long-term care, also a potential risk, is often completely overlooked.

When you fail to address your clients' LTC Planning needs, you either encourage them to ignore the issue, or you force them to turn to insurance agents as their source for advice. This does not serve your clients' best interest and could be detrimental to you. Because of your unique relationship with your client, you are in the best position to initiate LTC Planning and to make sure a solution is developed within the context of their personal and financial objectives.

But because so many financial professionals are not addressing this risk, millions of people who should plan ahead for long-term care are not, while others are being solicited by insurance agents, and purchasing an insurance product, rather than planning ahead based on their financial and estate planning needs. Why is this? Why are so many financial professionals failing to address the LTC Planning needs of their clients?

At least part of the problem is due to commonly held myths prevailing in our industry that lead financial professionals to avoid LTC Planning.

---

6 LTC Planning and Insurance Myths

Myth 1   If my client is wealthy enough to rely on their own assets to pay for long-term care, then that's what they should do.

Myth 2   My younger clients can ignore LTC Planning because they will not need long-term care anytime soon.

Myth 3   My younger clients will pay less if they postpone purchasing long-term care insurance.

Myth 4   As long as they are willing to pay the higher premiums, clients can wait to purchase long-term care insurance.

Myth 5   My younger clients are better off investing the money that would be used to pay for long-term care insurance.

Myth 6   I must be an LTC Planning expert before I can adequately address this issue with my clients.

Myth 1: If my client is wealthy enough to rely on their own assets to pay for long-term care, then that's what they should do.

Many financial professionals want their clients to view them as their primary resource—their first stop—for all financial advice. "Have a question about investments, taxes, insurance, estate planning or lifetime gifting? Come to me first. I can point you to the expert who can assist you." This level of service is invaluable for all clients, and particularly for wealthy clients. Yet, when it comes to addressing the LTC Planning needs of wealthy clients, many financial professionals believe that if clients *can* self-insure, they *should* self-insure.

Is this so different from saying that if a client *can* pay more taxes, they *should* pay more taxes? Our wealthy clients are delighted when we assist them with tax planning, and implement strategies to lower their tax bill; in turn, that money is invested to help them reach their financial goals. But we often fail to advise them that by paying insurance premiums, they could potentially avoid hundreds of thousands of dollars in long-term care expenses.

Some advisors might live by a rule such as, "Clients should not consider insuring for a long-term care risk if their liquid assets exceed $X million." But would your client agree if they knew that even a portfolio as high as $5 million could be depleted several years early if it were used to pay for years of long-term care? This scenario is feasible when you realize the national average cost of long-term care is about $60,000 per year, and the cost of care is predicted to rise much faster than the overall rate of inflation in the coming decades.

The *$5 Million Portfolio* chart on the next page shows what can happen to a $5 million portfolio that is required to generate a $208,000 annual income for a 60-year-old client and his spouse. The client plans to spend this income over the next 35 years of retirement. We assume a 5.3% after-tax return on investments, a 3% overall rate of inflation, and a 5% rate of inflation on long-term care expenses.

The **blue line** indicates the best-case scenario: no long-term care event, no money spent on LTC insurance premiums, and a portfolio that lasts through age 95. The **black line** shows what will happen if either the client or his spouse requires 10 years of long-term care at an average cost of $60,000 per year

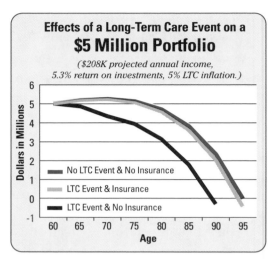

beginning one year into retirement. This long-term care event causes the portfolio to deplete a full six years earlier than planned. The **gray line** shows that a $5,000 annual investment in LTC insurance premiums restores all but one year of useful life to the portfolio—long-term care event or not.

What should your client do? Most financial professionals will agree that it is not our job to answer this question for our clients. It *is* our job, however, to educate our client about the dangers of failing to plan for long-term care, to present reasonable alternatives, and then let them decide which planning option to implement.

If 10 years of long-term care can shave 6 years off a $5 million portfolio, what happens to a smaller portfolio? It gets much worse. If, for example, your client's starting portfolio and income were half as much ($2.5 million portfolio and $104,000 annual income), their portfolio would be depleted by a full **10 years** earlier rather than 6 years—much earlier than planned if the same long-term care event occurred.

Our responsibility to each client is to understand that the acceptability of a catastrophic long-term care risk does not depend on the size of a client's portfolio alone. The *Comprehensive Planning Approach* considers the following:

- Cost of care, when and where the client may need it

- Client's projected level of spending in relation to their projected resources
- Number of years their resources need to last
- Client's personal tolerance for risk
- Assumptions about after-tax rates of return and inflation

This is the same information financial professionals use when analyzing retirement planning figures to project a client's capital needs. In fact, financial professionals can use their retirement planning software to quickly quantify and easily communicate the cost of introducing a 10-year long-term care event on a client's otherwise acceptable retirement plan. Input $60,000 per year in long-term care expenses (or a more appropriate average cost of care for the client's area) for 10 years with an inflation rate of 5% (or the most recent average rate of long-term care inflation). Review the age at which the money runs out and the revised probability of success. Then ask your client, "Is this scenario acceptable to you?" If not, then suggest they consider an alternative to self-insuring, such as passing the risk to an LTC insurance company.

Give your wealthy clients the advantage of knowing just how their portfolio will be impacted by a long-term care event. This level of service will not go unnoticed by your clients and their heirs.

Myth 2: *My younger clients can ignore LTC Planning because they will not need long-term care anytime soon.*

We normally don't hear about young people needing long-term care, but can it happen? What about your younger clients? Could they need long-term care as a result of an illness or accident? Of course they could.

Remember the celebrities who at early ages were disabled by an illness or accident? Annette Funicello was diagnosed with multiple sclerosis at age 45. Christopher Reeve suffered a paralyzing accident at age 43. Michael J. Fox was diagnosed with Parkinson's Disease at age 30.

Your younger clients could find themselves needing long-term care within a few months of leaving your office with their otherwise acceptable estate, retirement, or financial plan in hand, but without your recommendation that they develop a written plan to pay for long-term care. It's important to you and them that you warn them of the dangers and recommend an appropriate action. A financial professional once told me: "It's better to advise my clients to plan ahead for long-term care many years too early than one day too late."

Myth 3: *My younger clients will pay less if they postpone purchasing long-term care insurance.*

The two premium charts on the next page clearly illustrate that this belief is false. In this example, the average premium rates from two top-rated carriers are used to illustrate the premium at varying ages at the time the policy is issued. The **black bars** represent the annual premiums at the issue ages shown at the bottom of the charts. The **blue bars** represent the total cumulative premium dollars paid by the time the person reaches age 85.

Most financial professionals are surprised to see the similarity in total cumulative premiums paid over time, regardless of the age at which coverage is purchased. The **blue bars** show that cumulative premiums paid to age 85 vary between a low of $80,000 for a person being issued coverage at age 40 to a high of $89,640 for a person being issued coverage at age 75. This proves that not only do younger people never pay a higher cumulative premium than older people, but that younger clients actually pay less in cumulative premium.

You might argue that a younger person will pay more if we consider the time value of money. But this is also false because the younger person spreads the premium payments over more years. This results in the younger person's premium payments in later years being paid with much cheaper dollars.

The *"Today's Dollars"* chart discounts the cumulative dollars in the *"Nominal Dollars"* chart by an overall inflation rate of 3%. The chart illustrates that the present value of the 40-year-old's premium payments to age 85 is $43,367, while the 75-year-old's premium payments to age 85 is $69,795. This means that at virtually all ages, even factoring the time value of money, the younger a person is when they purchase LTC insurance, the lower the premium will be on both an annual and cumulative basis.

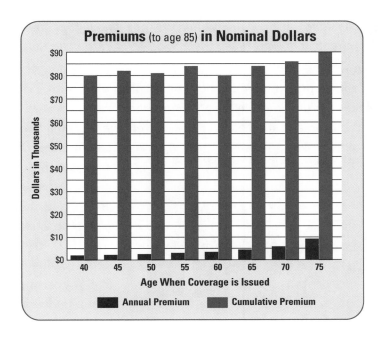

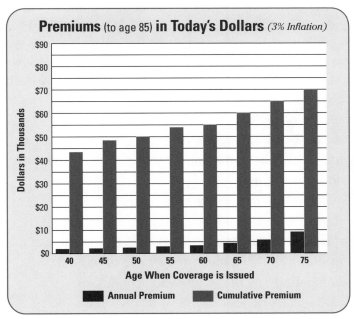

Myth 4: **As long as they are willing to pay the higher premiums, clients can wait to purchase long-term care insurance.**

While waiting until "the perfect age" to buy, your younger client could suffer a debilitating accident or be diagnosed with a disease that makes her uninsurable. The *"Underwriting Screen Failures"* chart shows the dramatic increases in the percentage of applicants who

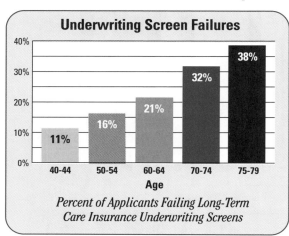

Underwriting Screen Failures

Percent of Applicants Failing Long-Term Care Insurance Underwriting Screens

fail to pass LTC insurance underwriting screens by age group. The number of people who fail to pass LTC insurance underwriting in the 60-64 year-old age group is nearly double that of the 40-44 year-old age group.

To better understand eligibility for LTC insurance and to explain how easily a person can become ineligible, simply show your client the following list and ask them, **"During the last 12 months did any of the following apply to you?"**

- The need for:
  - Assistance with any Activities of Daily Living (ADLs) including: eating, bathing, dressing, toileting, continence, and transferring
  - Home health care services
  - Care in a nursing home
  - A walker, wheelchair, medical appliance, kidney dialysis machine, or a manufactured source of oxygen
- Treatment for any of the following conditions:
  - Alzheimer's Disease
  - Acute and unspecified renal failure
  - Acute cerebral vascular disease
  - Chronic renal failure

- Cirrhosis of the liver
- Chronic memory loss
- Diabetes Mellitus with complications
- Mental retardation
- Multiple Sclerosis
- Paralysis
- Parkinson's Disease
- Schizophrenia and related disorders
- Senility and organic mental disorders
- Transient Ischemic Attack (TIA)

This list includes the many common, but not all disqualifying health conditions. While answering "Yes" to any of these conditions will most certainly disqualify your client for LTC insurance, answering "No" does not necessarily mean they will qualify. Long-term care insurance underwriting is performed on an individual basis and the underwriting process and standards vary from one insurance company to another. One carrier may accept your client, but only at a higher-than-preferred or standard premium rate, while another carrier may not accept their application at all. After your client submits an application and a more extensive underwriting process is completed, the carrier will determine eligibility *(see Chapter 13: The Application and Underwriting Process)*.

Myth 5: *My younger clients are better off investing the money that would be used to pay for long-term care insurance.*

This is only true if the client does not need long-term care for more than a few months during the decades she is investing the insurance premium. Let's compare whether a 40-year-old client should buy LTC insurance or invest the premium for 25 years. For comprehensive coverage and benefits that include inflation protection, her premium will be about $1,788 per year. She believes she can earn a 6% after-tax rate of return on her investment. The cost of care in her area is $158 per day. We assume the cost of long-term care will continue to grow at an average annual rate of 5%. Let's do the math. In 25 years, the invested premium at 6% interest will grow to $103,984. The cost of care in her area at 5% inflation will grow to $535 per day. So at the end of 25 years, when your client is about to turn 65, her investment account will cover 194 days ($103,983/$535) of long-term care. Put another way: after 25 years of investing the premium amount, your client's account will cover less than 7 months of long-term care.

And what if she has an accident or develops an illness and requires 10 years of long-term care beginning one year after she starts this investment account? Using national averages and a 5% inflation rate, this scenario would have 10 years of long-term care costing your younger client over $726,000.

What would this kind of catastrophe do to your 40-year-old's retirement plan—the path you drew to her financial security? Is your 40-year-old client willing to assume this risk? What about her family? You can't know, unless you ask. If she's like most clients at any age, she will automatically assume the risk unless you educate her about the consequences of her decision to her financial and estate plan and to her family. Initiating a proactive education is the process for helping her choose the LTC Planning option that is best for her.

Should your 40-year-old client eliminate LTC insurance as a consideration, or should she postpone considering LTC insurance until age 65? The answer to both questions is **NO** unless:

- She is willing to take the bet that she won't need long-term care for more than 7 months.
- She feels she can afford a several-hundred-thousand-dollar setback to her financial goals.
- She is willing to bet that she will never develop a debilitating accident or won't be diagnosed with a disease that will cause her to fail LTC insurance underwriting requirements *(see Myth 4)*.
- She has already developed health conditions that disqualify her for coverage.
- She has higher-priority risks that should be considered, and feels she cannot afford the LTC insurance premiums right now *(see Chapter 9: Is Long-Term Care Insurance Suitable for You?)*.
- Her risk tolerance philosophy dictates that she self-insure for insurable risks.

Myth 6: I must be an LTC Planning expert before I can adequately address this issue with my clients.

Do you have to be a CPA to discuss your client's general tax situation? Do you have to be an estate planning attorney to educate your client about the advantages and disadvantages of estate planning alternatives? Do you have to be a licensed insurance agent to recommend planning ahead with life or disability insurance? Of course not! But if you claim to assist your clients with comprehensive financial planning, and unless you clearly limit the advice you give your clients to very narrow and specific financial issues, your clients will justifiably rely on you to educate them about **ALL** risks to their financial goals and security, including the risk of long-term care. This is especially true if you are educating them about other insurable risks such as disability or early death.

The *Comprehensive Planning Approach* allows you to address this important issue with your clients at a level of expertise and involvement that is comfortable for you *(see Chapter 7: Planning Ahead Using the Comprehensive Planning Approach)*.

REPLACE THE MYTHS WITH THE FACTS

Myths are dangerous when they lead to misinformation and, in the case of LTC Planning, omission or avoidance on the part of financial professionals. The myths surrounding LTC Planning can lead to the demise of a carefully developed financial and estate plan and the collapse of a family's financial security.

In your business, success is not just a matter of delivering responsive service, strengthening the relationship, and attracting new clients. Success also comes from knowing that a financial plan, estate plan, or retirement plan has addressed all potential risks, including the often overlooked risk of long-term care.

KEY POINTS

LTC Planning and Insurance Myths

➤ Many financial professionals avoid the issue of LTC Planning because of commonly held myths. The two most prevalent myths pertain to age and net worth.

➤ Clients rely on their financial professional to identify risks to their portfolios and to their family and heirs, and to make recommendations to eliminate or decrease those risks.

➤ The younger you are when you purchase LTC insurance, the lower your *current* premium will be, and the lower your *cumulative* premium to life expectancy will be.

➤ Financial professionals do not need to become LTC Planning and Insurance experts to assist their clients with planning for long-term care. The *Comprehensive Planning Approach* allows you to choose your own level of expertise and involvement in the LTC Planning process.

Chapter 19

Interviews with Financial Professionals and Industry Experts

Many financial professionals and industry experts have been offering advice on the issue of LTC Planning for years.

The following interviews provide a variety of perspectives from a diverse range of financial professionals and industry experts. You will learn from these individuals that there are various perspectives and reasons for developing a written plan for long-term care.

Bob Bingham, CFP®
Principal of a Firm Serving High Net Worth Individuals

> *I used to tell my wealthier clients that they didn't need to include long-term care insurance in their consideration of LTC Planning options. But after seeing the true consequences of a long-term care event, I recommend it to virtually everybody.*

Bob Bingham is a Certified Financial Planner® with more than 20 years of experience. Based in San Francisco, he is an expert on wealth management for high net worth individuals. He is widely quoted in the national press, including *The Wall Street Journal*, *Barron's* and *BusinessWeek*.

Bingham, Osborn, and Scarborough has over $1.5 billion under management, serves over 600 clients and employs 30 people in 2 offices. Bob offers broad-based financial planning, including design and management of investment portfolios, and advice on a wide range of financial planning issues, such as investments, insurance, taxes, and more.

A large percentage of the firm's clients have the means to self-insure for long-term care, even against an extended stay in a first-class long-term care facility. Still, Bob raises the issue of LTC Planning with all his clients. He feels that even those who could self-insure should do so only after first considering the benefits of LTC insurance, purely from a financial planning perspective.

Q. Your clients are successful and financially savvy. Why do they need a professional adviser to help them make financial decisions?

A. People with substantial assets are confronted and bombarded with multiple financial decisions, choices that they need to make all the time. Even if they are very well informed about one or two areas of investment and financial planning, most do not have the time to become an expert in all areas of planning. We act as a Chief Financial Officer (CFO) for our clients, helping them see a coherent picture that includes all the pieces. Our job is to act as a guide, giving them the information and expertise they need to make decisions based on their individual circumstances and objectives. In order to achieve important goals, you need information and guidance. That's where we fit in—we are our clients' advocates in planning ahead for their best financial future.

Q. *Do you think that LTC planning is an important component of financial planning?*

A. Yes. Long-term care is the biggest risk in the portfolios of most upper-income people. We educate each of our clients about the risks of long-term care. They have planned ahead by investing in health insurance, homeowner's insurance, car, life and disability insurance. But in too many cases, they have no insurance for long-term care. It represents a huge risk for all people, whether they have substantial assets or not, because costs can easily run into the hundreds of thousands of dollars. We sometimes find that a new client is insuring a car worth $30,000, and going without insurance that poses a much larger risk of six-figures or more: long-term care.

Q. *How do you go about educating your clients?*

A. While it's true that most people are familiar with this topic, we inform our clients by using a process that educates them about the true potential financial risks of long-term care. We heavily emphasize the consequences of not planning ahead and what that could mean to them as an individual or family. Quite a few clients have given LTC planning some consideration before we address it. Most are familiar with the concept of LTC insurance. In general, people are more and more receptive to the idea that they need to plan ahead for long-term care. One reason is that baby boomers and middle-aged people in their 50s or 60s have often had the experience of caring for their own parents. I've had such an experience with my own father, and it certainly opened my eyes.

Q. *You work mainly with high net worth individuals. Don't they simply self-insure against the costs of long-term care?*

A. Some financial planners think that people with large portfolios should always self-insure. The conventional wisdom is that the wealthy do not need insurance. But it's not that difficult to be in a situation where you're spending over $250,000 per year on long-term care. That level of expense can quickly consume a portfolio that might otherwise be more productively employed.

Even if your assets are in the millions, you might still want to investigate LTC insurance to mitigate a financial risk that comes at the end of life and may cause consternation among children and heirs. Even if it covers only part of the actual expense, LTC insurance takes a lot of the pressure off people at a difficult time. Additionally, if people purchase coverage at a reasonably young age, and are in good health, LTC insurance is actually a good economic value, compared to many other types of insurance.

Q. *Please elaborate on this concept of "not automatically self-insuring."*

A. I used to tell my wealthier clients that they didn't need to include LTC insurance in their consideration of LTC Planning options. But after seeing the true consequences of a long-term care event, I recommend it to virtually everybody. I carefully explain the risks involved and challenge them to come up with a comfortable scenario without LTC insurance. Very few want to face that challenge, once they're familiar with the risks involved.

I also tell them, "Don't necessarily insure the full amount." If you estimate costs of $100,000 per year for the quality of care you desire, maybe you should insure for about half of that amount and cover the rest out-of-pocket.

Q. *The long-term care costs you mention are quite high compared to the national average of about $60,000 per year.*

A. I have first-hand experience and strong feelings about this because of what I went through with my father. I found it was very easy to rack up costs of over $250,000 per year if you were arranging care for someone who needed a professional attendant 24 hours a day in order to stay at home.

My father recently died in Cleveland. He had been in an "Assisted Living" apartment for years but eventually came to the point where he needed help with things like dressing or making sure he didn't fall. One option was to move him into a nursing home. Although that was the least expensive choice, we wanted him to be as comfortable as possible during his last years of life.

He didn't have any exotic debilitating disease, and we decided to pay for his care in the apartment where he had lived for years. We arranged for private caregivers to come in 24 hours a day. In Cleveland, private caregivers charge about $16 per hour. With 24-hour, round-the-clock care, plus rent for his apartment and other medical expenses, we faced costs of $250,000 per year, or close to $1 million over a period of four years. Although costs like this are far above the average, situations like this are not as rare as most of us think.

Q. *We've talked about high net worth individuals. What about people who have less substantial assets?*

A. Long-term care insurance is not cheap, and the hardest decisions about whether or not to purchase coverage are for those who are right on the edge of affordability. The most vulnerable people, in some respects, are middle class couples. A single person can always sell the house to fund long-term care. But if one partner in a couple has to go into a facility, the other usually wants to remain at home. That means they can't sell their house and are dependent on money in their investment portfolio. I personally believe that people with average means should at least investigate LTC insurance. The decision to purchase coverage or not will depend on many factors, including their age and health. People of average means who invest in coverage at a young enough age may be able to afford coverage, especially if they are still in good health.

Q. *Any other tips for people who are considering LTC insurance?*

A. The most important consideration is the financial strength of the insurance company being considered. There are big differences between companies in this market. Financial professionals should locate an LTC Planning and Insurance expert who stays abreast of the most qualified insurance companies.

We need to remember that it can easily be 30 years between the time you purchase a policy and the time you need it. You want a company that will be around when you need it. I wouldn't consider buying from an insurance company that is small and unknown, even if their premiums were lower. I would only consider large, highly rated companies with a long history in the LTC insurance industry.

Linda Silveria, Estate Planning Attorney
Certified Estate Planning Specialist

Learning how to use the "Comprehensive Planning Approach" to long-term care made me realize the importance of planning in advance for both my clients AND my own family.

Linda Silveria is an attorney in private practice in San Jose, CA. For the past 25 years, she has devoted her practice to issues involving estate planning, probate and trust law. In 1991 she was certified as a specialist in Estate Planning, Probate and Trust Law by the California Board of Legal Specialization of the State Bar of California. Linda is a member of the Trusts and Estate section of the State Bar of California and is a member of the Estate Planning section of the Silicon Valley Bar Association. She is also a member of the Santa Clara County Bar Association. Linda is a frequent lecturer on estate planning topics to the general public.

Q. *How do you go about approaching the subject of LTC Planning with your clients?*

A. Having recently gone through training to learn the *Comprehensive Planning Approach* to Long-Term Care, I now make it a point during my estate planning work with my clients to ask them what their plan is for long-term care. The training made me realize the importance of making sure each client understands and analyzes the 4 ways to pay for care and to develop their written plan in advance. The training also personally motivated me to deliberately choose an option for my own family. I realized that if my husband or I developed a serious illness, we needed to have a plan in place that had been communicated to the rest of our family.

Q. *So your approach revolves around a discussion about each of the 4 options to pay for care?*

A. Yes, but it may not be a deep discussion about each option. For example, most people are not comfortable with the thought of relying on their family or relying on the welfare program. I assist clients from their unique standpoint—in other words, I help them understand the implications of each option for their own family. Many times, the option that seems most appropriate has me referring them to another specialist in a particular area. For instance, we don't offer LTC insurance, so we refer the client to an LTC Planning and Insurance expert if that's the option they want to consider.

Q. *Let's get more specific about this process you use to educate clients about LTC Planning.*

A. I begin by explaining that in the past, the most common option was to rely on a family member. But the family structure is different now. Analyzing this option usually revolves around whether or not the children would be able to assist with their care. Many grown children are geographically separated from their parents. In addition, two incomes are commonly needed to support families: the option of leaving the workforce to care for a parent may not be feasible. Once they understand how their children's lives might be affected by their need for care, most of my clients are not interested in deliberately relying on a family member. But some of my clients may be interested in exploring this option. If so, we then discuss the family's specific situation to see if this is a serious option. For example, we might discuss whether or not the children have children of their own; their children's employment situation; and whether or not the children own their home. In other words, from a realistic standpoint, we thoroughly analyze the children's ability to provide care. In the end, most people realize that children do not have the resources to provide for their parents' care, from either a financial or a time standpoint.

Q. *What about the welfare program?*

A. That's the second and probably most confusing option for paying for care. In 2006, Congress passed the Deficit Reduction Act, making it more difficult for individuals to qualify for welfare. I believe this trend will continue as Congress attempts to balance the budget.

Using welfare is a rather difficult and complicated process because it generally involves transferring assets out of the name of the elder person and into the names of the children. This is an emotional discussion for the elders because they've worked hard for their assets and the idea of spending those assets on long-term care, or giving them away, creates a great deal of stress.

Quality of care in welfare approved nursing homes can also be an issue. As our country continues to experience budgetary problems and as the population continues to age, it is generally believed that the quality of care provided by welfare will decline.

But if a person has developed health problems and has no other options, welfare may be the only option. In my practice, I can assist families in qualifying for the welfare program if other options are exhausted or limited. Even though welfare is not a very attractive option, neither is paying large amounts of hard-earned money each month to a nursing home for the care of an ill spouse. And if the need for care depletes the couple's assets, how will the well spouse pay for *their* future care? This is why long-term care is such a complicated dilemma.

Q. *Do you have clients who want to use the third option — Personal Assets?*

A. Yes, some of my clients decide that if they need long-term care, they will simply use their assets. This means that they would first exhaust their investments, then the house would be sold and the equity would be used to pay for care. Many times this works out. For example, one of my female clients entered a nursing home in her 80's and her assets were still paying for her care at her death at age 105. This worked well for her because she was single. Another client, a couple, made the decision to rely on their own assets and it didn't work out as well: The wife entered a facility and still needed care 15 years later. The husband was dismayed that so much of their net worth had been used to pay for her care and is in the situation I just mentioned: Concerned about where the money will come from to pay for his care if he needs assistance. When considering using our own assets to pay for care, we need to look at that option from all angles.

Q. *Do you have an example of a client who chose the fourth option—long-term care insurance?*

A. That's the option we personally chose for our family. I recently met with a widowed client who made the same choice. During my review of her estate plan, she told me she had purchased long-term care insurance when she was about 80 years old. It became clear during our discussion that her motivation was her 3 children: It was very important to her that she not be a burden on her children. She stated that the premiums were quite high but she has sufficient income to pay the premiums. She also stated that her biggest regret was that she did not purchase the policy when she was younger.

Q. *What is the most important advice you have for people about the issue of long-term care?*

A. To plan in advance. To not wait until your options are limited or until a crisis develops. The importance of planning in advance can't be overemphasized.

Larry Pon, CPA
A CPA's Perspective

Long-term care is a family affair.
Children should assist their parents in understanding
the implications of needing care. Parents should plan
so they don't become a burden to their children.

Larry Pon is a CPA with a solo practice in the heart of Silicon Valley, California. His clients include individuals and small business owners. A typical service might involve a Silicon Valley entrepreneur whose company is being bought out and who seeks help in calculating and/or minimizing the tax bill from the sale of the business. Other common services include reducing the tax bill on the sale of real estate. Recognizing that tax planning is just one piece of a larger puzzle, Larry likes to work collaboratively with the other professionals involved in his clients' financial and estate planning.

Q. *Long-term care insurance is sometimes called a "tax-favored form of insurance." As a CPA, do you agree with that assessment?*

A. The tax benefits of LTC insurance can be good for some people, especially for business owners. As of 2003, companies with employees are able to write off 100 percent of their LTC insurance premiums as an above-the-line deduction. Even individual taxpayers can deduct premiums if their total medical expenses are above 7.5 percent of their adjusted gross income. In contrast, the premiums for many other types of individually issued insurance aren't tax deductible at all.

Q. *What about the benefits a policyholder receives if she needs long-term care? Are they considered taxable income?*

A. The benefits in tax-qualified LTC insurance policies are generally tax-free. So while business owners who purchase coverage for employees are able to enjoy a tax deduction, the employee is not required to report the coverage as a benefit because benefits received from an LTC insurance policy are not subject to taxes if and when they collect on the policy. It can be a very big incentive for many employees, and can help employers retain good employees because they're offering a benefit that most companies do not offer. Of course, each person's tax situation should be reviewed by a tax professional since tax issues related to long-term care can be complex.

Q. *Do you recommend that your clients buy coverage because of the tax advantages?*

A. That depends on a cost-benefit analysis that varies for each individual. But for the majority, the tax break is not the first benefit people look for when it comes to LTC insurance. Most of the people who buy coverage do so to keep from becoming a burden to their children. Another common scenario is when a client's children decide to buy coverage for their parents. The children pay the premium, with the objective of having their parents remain at home, or at least move to a facility where they feel comfortable, rather than relying on the welfare program, Medicaid (MediCal in California).

Q. *Why is this such an important area of financial and estate planning? And how should people go about getting educated about LTC Planning?*

A. Long-term care is a family affair. Children should assist their parents in understanding the implications of needing care. Parents should plan so they don't become a burden to their children. The best way to learn more about this issue is to see an LTC Planning and Insurance expert.

Q. *Have you had any personal experiences with clients who choose LTC insurance coverage and use it?*

A. I had an experience just recently that shows the value of the coverage when it is used. A client purchased LTC insurance at the age of 80. She later needed care and went into a facility and stayed for about two years before she died. Even though she purchased coverage at such an advanced age, she still received benefits that were far greater than the premiums paid.

Don St. Clair, CFP ®

President, Financial Planning Association, Northern California

Unfortunately, the LTC Planning process is heavily influenced by the insurance industry. People need to realize that long-term care planning doesn't necessarily include "insurance." This is a financial and estate planning process.

Don St. Clair has been serving the financial planning needs of individuals and their families since 1990. He has lectured throughout California at state universities, community colleges, district offices and campuses. His straightforward style of communication coupled with his extensive investment and financial planning knowledge make him unique in his ability to successfully convey difficult concepts. A Certified Financial Planner®, with a Bachelor of Science Degree in Finance, Don is committed to providing state-of-the-art financial planning, investment management, and retirement planning services designed to help build and preserve the financial wealth of his clients. He currently serves as President of the Financial Planning Association of Northern California.

Q. Don, can you tell us your philosophy when it comes to financial planning?

A. I don't think it's an accident that people who plan their finances, by-in-large end up financially better off than those who don't. The primary purpose of financial planning should be to determine the very best course of action for the client. And this should be done before any implementation takes place. I say this because too often, financial planning is positioned as a loss-leader – a sales tool used to capture investment assets and sell insurance. But in order to benefit from the financial planning process, you actually have to go through it – not be fooled by some sales-pitch disguised as financial planning.

Q. In your financial planning practice, do you have very many clients who ask you about LTC insurance?

A. Unfortunately, the LTC Planning process is heavily influenced by the insurance industry. People need to realize that long-term care planning doesn't necessarily include "insurance." This is a financial and estate planning process.

Q. So you see it as a planning process on several levels?

A. Yes. Long-term care is more than just a money issue. Anyone who's had personal experience with the issue will tell you that money was only one of the many factors they had to deal with.

Q. Do you find that a lot of the people who bring up LTC insurance have had personal experiences with this issue?

A. There's almost a line of demarcation between those who have had personal experiences and those who haven't. That might sound terribly obvious, but the people who have had a long-term care experience find it very difficult to convey how life-altering it can be to those who haven't experienced it. The difficulty for a financial planner is that people who have no personal experience are often times not open to a conversation about the topic in the first place. And without a conversation, there is no planning – leaving the majority of people exposed to this potentially catastrophic event.

Q. Is LTC insurance part of your planning checklist?

A. Not so much the insurance, because we don't recommend that everyone purchase LTC insurance. But we do explore the issue in terms of *"Who would provide the care? How would we pay for the care? Would we have to sell the home? How would needing long-term care affect our children; or our spouse's ability to continue working; or their ability to continue enjoying personal activities?"* So we talk about the threat of needing long-term care as it relates to the financial *and* life plans of our clients. And while we use the framework of our client's retirement income and monthly cash flows as a starting point for the conversation, we generally end up talking more about the non-financial issues associated with long-term care.

Q. *Do you feel that most financial planners are familiar with this topic and are bringing it up with their clients?*

A. I think that more financial planners are becoming familiar with the topic. And yes, I do think that they're bringing it up with their clients. But the statistics show that there isn't much follow through happening after they bring it up. I think that's because there's a stigma associated with this issue of planning for long-term care, one that relates to the fact that we're talking about an insurable event. Unfortunately, many financial planners are uncomfortable talking about insurance because they don't want to be seen as pushing insurance. I say that this is unfortunate because in the end it's the client who suffers from the planners' lack of forthright expression. I mentioned before that many people are not even open to the conversation, so our task is not always an easy one. My hope would be that planners begin to take a stronger stand with their clients regarding this issue. If not us, then who will educate them about the need to plan?

Q. *Elaborate on that "insurance stigma" comment. How can that be solved?*

A. Financial Planners need to educate all their clients about LTC Planning, but realize "insurance" will only be appropriate at certain times. The best approach is to develop a relationship with an LTC Planning and Insurance expert, who works with clients the same way we do: with an educational, consultative approach.

Q. *When it comes to a hierarchy of risks, where would you place LTC insurance from the standpoint of importance?*

A. I think that's the whole point of the exercise of financial planning. It's the exploration of the client's financial situation, their options for taking action, the risks involved, and the probabilities for success. So for a working couple with children in grade school, would I place LTC insurance ahead of disability and life insurance? Of course not! But the same couple approaching age 55, with their children grown and their retirement almost fully funded? That's a totally different story.

Q. *Do you think there is an ideal age for people to be taking a look at LTC insurance?*

A. No. The evaluation is situational, and while age is certainly part of what makes up someone's situation, it isn't the only consideration. I don't know of any other way to evaluate this than to play out the scenario. That's the only way I've found to even begin taking into account all the variables that need to be considered. So we hold a *fire-drill* of sorts and we say "okay, tomorrow when you wake up one of you will be in need of care – what do we need to do?"

Q. *Do you have any thoughts on the amount of assets a person should have before they rely on their own assets to pay for care?*

A. My understanding is that the people who are the primary buyers of LTC insurance – at least today – are folks who **could afford** to self-insure. In other words, they have the money and could sustain a catastrophic long-term care event without threatening their assets or running out of money. For these people it's not a matter of whether they can afford to self-insure, it's a matter of **why** they would. They say "would I rather pay a few hundred bucks a month today, or risk having to come up with several hundred thousand tomorrow?" Unfortunately, many folks don't have the luxury of being able to readily afford either outcome – buying insurance or self-insuring. Some people can't afford either the premium, or the care if needed – but that's what Medicaid (welfare) is for. Still others find themselves able to afford the insurance premium, but no way could they afford the care if it were needed. Unfortunately, some of these people are playing Russian roulette with their financial future.

Q. *From a personal standpoint, is LTC insurance something that you believe in? Have you had any personal experiences with relatives or friends who needed long-term care?*

A. I do feel strongly about this issue, and I do believe in insuring risks that are, well, insurable. But I try not to project my own biases on my clients. If someone really **can** afford to self-insure; or they really do have family that will step in and provide care if needed; or they will readily qualify for Medicaid; ***and*** they don't want to plan for their possible long-term care needs through insurance – then it's not my job to convince them otherwise. My role is to make certain that my clients know the risks, and plan accordingly.

As for personal experiences – my father was hospitalized for about three weeks prior to his death. His oncologist, a wonderfully caring woman, approached me one day to say "we've got a problem, your dad needs skilled nursing, but he's too well to stay here (at the hospital). On the other hand, since he probably won't live another month, he's too sick to go to a skilled nursing facility." I was in my mid-twenties and just starting my career, so I knew nothing of the rules of the situation he was in. The next day I ran into the oncologist in the hallway. She was smiling, and pleased to announce that my father had developed pneumonia. At first I didn't understand her enthusiasm, but she explained "Now we can keep him here, where he can continue to be cared for." The truth is, I didn't realize until years later that we came very close to facing a long-term care situation.

James Phillips, Estate Planning Attorney
Estate and Tax Planning

> *Unfortunately, in my practice I've had to personally assist clients whose children had become more concerned for their inheritance than they were for mom or dad's care. A plan for long-term care can help to guard against this greed/fear factor.*

James Phillips is an attorney who has been specializing in estate planning, trusts and related matters since 1980. In addition to his law degree, he has a Masters in Law Taxation. His family has a two-generation legal tradition in Northern California. His father was Alameda Superior Court Judge George W. Phillips. James grew up with an elderly grandmother who had a profound influence on his values, especially his interest in issues relating to older people and long-term care.

Q. Is LTC Planning an important aspect of estate planning?

A. It's on the list of areas that I discuss with all new clients who come to me for estate planning. I ask how they plan to pay for long-term care in a nursing home, assisted living community, or their own home. Most people have not thought the matter through. But since people who come to me are in a "planning ahead" mode of thinking, I think it's important to make them aware of this issue. LTC Planning is something that my clients are usually glad we discussed.

Q. Do you go over the various options available for paying for long-term care?

A. I think every client should make an informed and analytical decision about planning for the payment of long-term care services. So, yes, I explain the four planning options available to them: rely on family, welfare (Medicaid or Medi-Cal in California), their assets, or insurance.

Q. *How do your clients choose the right option?*

A. We talk about how each option fits in. For example, to rely on their assets, clients need sufficient assets and income to provide comfortably for home health care or long-term care in a nursing home or assisted living community. Only the fortunate few fall into this category. But even my clients with significant wealth do not want to spend their after-tax income on a prolonged need for long-term care.

Medicaid, or MediCal as we call it in California, does pay for long-term care in a nursing home, but rarely includes home health care. I make sure that my clients understand that the safety net offered by Medicaid provides for long-term care only in Medicaid-certified facilities and in a non-private-room. To qualify for government assistance, clients must pass three tests: an income test, an asset test, and a wealth-transfer test. Most of my clients would flunk the income and asset test because they own more than Medicaid allows. If they pass assets over to their heirs, they will fail the transfer test that defines the time period and the manner in which assets can be transferred in order to qualify for government aid.

Most of my clients would rather choose the non-welfare options available to them. The Medicaid option is simply a "problematic solution." If they do not want to rely on their assets or rely on their family, I actively recommend LTC insurance as the option of choice.

Q. *How should they go about investigating coverage?*

A. I tell clients that they should work with a certified independent LTC Planning and Insurance expert who will provide them with an education about long-term care, followed by quotes and benefit information for LTC insurance from several top-rated carriers, not just one. With those quotes and a detailed explanation of the benefits, they have the information they need to decide whether or not coverage makes sense for them as a solution for planning ahead for long-term care.

Q. Elaborate on LTC insurance as a consideration from an estate planning perspective.

A. If clients can afford the premiums, there are three compelling reasons to buy LTC insurance. The first is to avert the risk of significant economic harm from uninsured costs. I've seen large estates decimated by the cost of long-term care where there was no LTC insurance in force. Second, for married couples there is enormous emotional stress associated with worrying about payment and the quality of available services for the care of a spouse in need of care. Owning LTC insurance allows a family to significantly reduce both the economic stress of a long-term care event, as well as the emotional stress. Third, there is always the risk that whoever is in charge of your finances will be so consumed by fear or greed about their future inheritance that they may not be willing to allocate your funds for the high quality of care that you had planned to receive. Unfortunately, in my practice I've had to personally assist clients whose children had become more concerned for their inheritance than they were for mom or dad's care. A plan for long-term care can help to guard against this greed/fear factor.

Q. So you see part of the planning process as being about protecting the "relationship" between family members?

A. Yes I do. The impact of caregiving can include strained relationships with a spouse and/or children. We need to remember that there are emotional costs associated with this issue of long-term care.

Chad Burton, CFP ®
Fee-Based Financial Planner

*We have only a few risks that have the potential
of totally wiping out our financial security,
and long-term care is on that short list.
This issue is a top priority in our practice –
an area that MUST be discussed with all clients.*

Chad Burton is a Certified Financial Planner® and CEO of New Focus Financial Group with offices in Vancouver, Washington; Larkspur, California; and San Mateo, California. Chad is a fee-based advisor providing both financial planning and money management services. He entered financial planning in 1993 by joining his grandfather, Robert Finch, and was immediately trained in retirement and estate planning for his grandfather's older clientele.

Chad is host of a live call-in show that delivers current stock market news and up to date financial planning topics. Chad is also a frequent television guest on the popular financial show "Rob Black and Your Money" and "Ask the Experts."

Q. *Do you actively bring up the subject of LTC Planning with your clients?*

A. Absolutely! When I started in this business the average age of my grandfather's clientele was just under 70. About 3 years into the business it seemed we had a regular flow of calls from clients worried about how they would pay for their ill spouse's care at home or in a facility. Unfortunately, these people had to search for a way to avoid spousal impoverishment and that limited their options for the type of care they could receive. It also became apparent to me very early in my practice that single people or widows had very few options but to deplete their wealth when faced with long- term care costs. Back then, we were "putting out fires" for many clients, due to their lack of planning. Our service now includes discussing LTC Planning with our clients to prevent those "fires."

Q. How do you go about approaching the subject?

A. We use a visual example to create a hypothetical 5-year need for long-term care beginning in a client's mid to late 70's. This process clearly points to the need to develop a written plan for long-term care, and many times that plan includes insurance.

Q. Why do you think most people are not planning ahead for long-term care?

A. I don't think most people really understand that this is an important financial and estate planning issue. In decades past, people received their care at home from a family member, usually a spouse, daughter, or daughter-in-law. But due to the trends of two-career households and families living in different regions of the country, a widespread need is occurring: the need for care by *paid* caregivers rather than family members. These trends are expanding the overall awareness of the need to plan for long-term care.

Q. Do you think most financial planners are addressing LTC Planning with their clients?

A. I think it is becoming much more common due to liability issues. All financial planners should address the topic because long-term care costs are one of the biggest risks facing a family's financial security. Fortunately, most advisors realize that planning for long- term care is part of their professional responsibility. Unfortunately, many advisors experience problems when it comes to follow through and implementation. It is important for advisors to locate an LTC planning and Insurance expert for their clients – one who can assist them in implementing a written plan for long-term care.

Q. Tell me more about your "5 Year Scenario". That sounds like a pretty good preliminary needs analysis process.

A. Yes, it is. The scenario illustrates a significant change in lifestyle for the surviving spouse in most cases, reducing the amount earmarked for a secure lifestyle for the healthy spouse or depleting an inheritance set aside for children. Once we go through this very basic needs analysis and answer some basic questions for the client, we then refer the client to an LTC Planning expert.

Q. *Where do you rank LTC Planning in importance in the over-all financial planning process?*

A. We have only a few risks that have the potential of totally wiping out our financial security, and long-term care is on that short list. I rank a discussion about this issue near the top of the list of areas that **MUST** be discussed with clients. I even encourage wealthy people to have an open mind about considering LTC insurance as part of their plan, so that their heirs make health care decisions based on quality of care rather than on the size of the estate that will be left for the heirs after paying for care. Those requiring long-term care are often required to turn over financial and health care decisions to loved ones. Unfortunately, I have seen too many health care decisions made by heirs based on what they would inherit instead of finding the best option of care for the one in need of care. When money's involved, I've seen people justify almost anything.

Q. *Do you think the government does a good job of educating the public about the issue of planning ahead for long-term care?*

A. We need more in the form of education from federal and state governments because too many people mistakenly assume they are covered for quality long-term care by the government. Much of this misunderstanding has to do with a lack of clarity in communicating the government's limited role regarding payment for long-term care.

Q. *What about incentives for planning ahead for long-term care? Does our government do enough in the form of incentives?*

A. I see incremental improvements in this area, but the pace is frustrating. For example, tax code legislation to provide ***meaningful*** tax breaks for LTC insurance premiums should be passed immediately on both a federal and state(s) level.

Q. *Do you have a certain amount of assets in dollars that you think a person should have before they automatically eliminate LTC insurance as an option for their LTC Plan?*

A. No matter what a person's net worth is, everyone needs a written plan for long-term care: One major health problem can put a wealthy person right back into the middle or lower class very quickly. So the answer is "no": Those who can afford to self-insure should still consider the insurance. As I mentioned, an important aspect of LTC insurance is that it helps to ensure that health care decisions made by heirs are based on obtaining the best level of care possible rather than maximizing an inheritance. In addition to encouraging clients to evaluate LTC insurance as an option, I also recommend that they add language to their living trusts that instruct their successor trustees as to the level of care they desire.

Q. *What do you think is the most important aspect of an LTC insurance policy?*

A. I think there are two aspects of insurance that are equally important. One is the ability to be able to stay at home for care. LTC insurance is many times thought of as "nursing home insurance", but the home care aspect is designed to keep people out of a facility. Most people would like to stay in their own home as long as possible, and LTC insurance is one way to make sure that option is available. The second feature is the care coordinator benefit of a policy. This feature can assist families in locating quality providers of care. This feature may become the most beneficial aspect of all—freeing families from searching for quality providers of care during the time of need, and allowing them to focus on providing emotional care.

Dr. James Knickman, Ph.D.

*A Leader in the Development of the
Public/Private Partnerships for Long-Term Care*

> *Long-term care insurance, an example
> of a private sector solution, is working,
> but we need more government education
> about the issue of long-term care.*

Dr. James Knickman, Ph.D., is Vice President of Research and Evaluation at the Robert Wood Johnson Foundation, which launched the respected program for public/private partnerships in LTC insurance called the "Partnership Programs." An economist by training, Dr. Knickman was the Regents Lecturer at the University of California. Long-term care insurance Partnership Programs match private contributions with public funds on a dollar-to-dollar basis to pay for long-term care costs. The Partnership Program is explained in *Chapter 16.*

Q. Are our current systems for long-term care financing and delivery doing a good job?

A. Our current systems are not exactly a national embarrassment but they let too many people fall through the cracks. They are also too confusing. Many people can't figure out how to get the services they need. In about 45 of the 50 states, we are a humane society in that you will get care, even if you run out of money. The tough question for public policy is how will the system develop in coming years? Will we expand services for the truly poor, or try some universal system that gives coverage to the middle class and even the wealthy?

Q. Please elaborate on the options for financing long-term care.

A. There are two revenue streams for financing the cost of long-term care: public and private. The public stream is Medicaid, our backup system for the truly poor, or for middle-class people who become impoverished due to the high cost of long-term care. Most people start out as private-pay, paying for the costs of long-term care out-of-pocket. Once they "spend-down" their assets, they go on Medicaid. If you have no resources and start off as a Medicaid patient, it may be hard to get into a good nursing home. The better homes are hoping you'll be private-pay for at least a year or two prior to going on Medicaid. These nursing homes use a strategy of servicing a blend of Medicaid and private-pay patients, so that they are able to remain fiscally solvent.

In terms of private financing for long-term care services, we have a decentralized delivery system which is very private-sector oriented. Even the non-profits in the field act like for-profit corporations. That kind of market-oriented delivery system has a negative and a positive side. The negative side is that the system is not as "touchy-feely" or as humane as some might want. On the positive side, it is an efficient system in that it responds quickly to the market.

Long-term care insurance, an example of a private sector solution, is working, but we need more government education about the issue of long-term care. This would create more innovative responses from the industry and more interest from consumers.

Q. Where are the costs of long-term care heading?

A. The costs of nursing homes and home care will continue to rise sharply, and in some years, at a much greater rate than the general rate of inflation. It's been difficult in both the public and private sector to keep a solid lid on costs. A high rate of inflation will create real problems if it compounds over twenty or thirty years. But, as an economist by training, I don't see that trend continuing indefinitely.

For example, my brother recently bought a house in Florida and told me enthusiastically, "Real estate prices are up 15% per year, and maybe that will last for the rest of our lives!" But prices can't go up like that forever. The upward trend will slow at some point, normally due to supply and demand issues, and average inflation will be at a much lower percentage.

In other words, the market works. We are going to see technologies and innovations in long-term care services and delivery that keep the costs from escalating out of control. In my opinion, it will not be so much a matter of controlling costs as it will be transforming the delivery system. Instead of making the cost of beds in a skilled nursing home go way down, we'll see new communities of care evolve to offer alternative services at a lower cost. That's what people want. It's already beginning to happen. For example, the decline in use of nursing homes is a mirror image of the rising popularity of assisted living communities.

Technology will also play a major role in helping elders stay independent. Surveillance technology for monitoring vital signs could reduce the cost of care, and high-tech wheelchairs with onboard computers to help with stability could make disabled people much more mobile.

Q. *Who faces the greatest financial risk from the high cost of long-term care?*

A. The people in the middle are most at risk. The poor can be taken care of by Medicaid. The wealthy can pay for their own care even if they don't purchase LTC insurance. It's the people in the middle who are caught short.

Take a couple with a modest amount of assets, say $100,000. They don't want to spend money on LTC insurance because they have other financial responsibilities that seem to take precedence. They have medical bills and maintenance on the home. Important questions are ahead for them, such as "What will the wife do if she outlives the husband?" They don't know how long they'll live, or how many years of long-term care services they might need. And because of all these uncertainties, and the fact that LTC insurance premiums represent such a large percentage of their income and assets, they default to having no plan.

Q. *Are the baby boomers really a demographic time bomb as some experts say?*

A. Yes. From a macro-economic perspective, 76 million boomers are going to challenge the long-term care system. If changes aren't made, this generation will overwhelm the Medicaid program. The whole issue of who is and is not being taken care of will gain prominence as the boomers move further into retirement and old age. The salience of the issue in the media will increase. As a nation, we have the resources to solve this problem, but we have not yet made the tough choices about how to marshal these resources.

An interesting demographic change is taking place. If you define dependents as people who don't work, we will have no more dependents as a percentage of population in 2030 than we did in 1960. In the 1960s, we had more children and fewer elders. But that ratio will be reversed in coming years.

We'll face three economic shocks in the next two decades. One is the cost of prescription drugs, which recently created a huge national debate. The second area is the continually rising cost of health care services not covered by Medicare, including doctor and hospitalization care. And the third, by far the biggest shock, will be the cost of long-term care.

When it comes to long-term care, the debate will be (1) do you want to force people to pre-fund their own care, through some sort of mandatory contribution into a private account or (2) do you rely on the current system—a public, pay-as-you-go system where each generation finances care for its elders?

Q. *Which method of funding long-term care seems most viable?*

A. Personally, I think pre-funding is the only realistic answer. I just do not see the government stepping in and funding a multi-billion dollar entitlement for long-term care. We are running deficits now, but even in times of surplus there are competing priorities. I am not sure that most Americans are eager to be taxed at higher and higher rates for public services. If you ask, "Do you want lower taxes now or public long-term care benefits thirty years from now?" most people are going to want lower taxes. That's just the way it is.

One solution might be mandatory savings accounts for long-term care. If everyone was required to put a certain percentage of income, say 1.5%, into a private, personal, unshared account, and if they began contributing in their 20s, most people would have enough money accumulated to buy their own paid-up LTC insurance policy as they reached their middle age years.

By forcing people to contribute, in effect, you are raising their taxes. But even relatively conservative people, such as Pete Peterson (author of *Gray Dawn* and a very influential voice in the long-term care debate), recommend mandatory pre-funding. It's a way of forcing people to put away a little each week. Those who oppose tax increases on principle are willing to consider mandatory pre-funding because the funds invested stay private. They go into your personal account, not into a common fund.

Q. *Where do the Partnership Program policies fit into this debate?*

A. Our feeling was that we already have some share of Medicaid dollars going to support long-term care for middle-class people who were independent until they became old and frail. Why not try to blend these public dollars with what people now spend out-of-pocket to develop more comprehensive LTC insurance and create some incentives for people to pre-fund? We came up with one idea: "quid pro quo," or dollar-for-dollar matching. Whatever dollar amount of insurance benefits you use up front, you automatically get to keep, and receive Medicaid benefits after your private long-term care coverage runs out. There are probably lots of other ways to blend public and private funding more efficiently than we do now, but this was a good start. The point is to use public dollars as an incentive to encourage middle-class people to invest in their own long-term care financing.

Q. *How successful have the Partnership Programs been?*

A. The Partnerships are alive and healthy. But they reach only a small percentage of the population. They are doing well, but not reaching down into the levels of the middle class we really hope to engage.

Q. *Is the Partnership going to grow beyond the states that currently have them?*

A. Yes, other states will be offering a Partnership Program. Our model has not completely solved the problem, but we're still convinced that some variant of our approach, some way to combine and leverage public and private spending, is the solution for financing long-term care. People who are opposed to public funding will have to agree that we can get more leverage from Medicaid money by using some portion of it to encourage private pre-funding by the middle class.

Stephen A. Moses
President, Center for Long-Term Care Reform, Inc.

The Coming Challenge of Long-Term Care

*If the baby boom is the Titanic,
long-term care is the iceberg.*

Stephen A. Moses is President of the Center for Long-Term Care Reform, Inc., a nonpartisan think tank and public policy organization dedicated to "ensuring quality long-term care for all Americans." For published articles, reports and speeches, see the Center's website at *www.centerltc.org*.

Q. How would you describe the challenge of long-term care?

A. If the baby boom is the Titanic, long-term care is the iceberg. Nearly 40 years of easy access to Medicaid nursing home benefits and, more recently, long-term home care from Medicare, have lulled the American public into a false sense of security about long-term care. Today, Medicaid is on the verge of bankruptcy and suffers from a dismal reputation for problems of access, quality, reimbursement, discrimination, and institutional bias. Medicare's fiscal crisis is closing like a vise and the program has already cut back on home care costs with draconian vigor. Can you imagine what these programs are going to look like, if they even exist, in 20 or 30 years when the boomers start to need long-term care? It will not be pretty!

Q. How do you see your organization, the Center for Long-Term Care Reform, Inc., helping with the problem of long-term care?

A. Our only hope to prepare for the demographic onslaught of exponentially greater long-term care needs is to wean the public off the expectation that Medicaid, Medicare or any future publicly financed program is going to pay for long-term custodial care. We must offer a better and affordable alternative to people when they are still young, healthy, and affluent enough to qualify for it. That is the mission of the Center for Long-Term Care Reform, Inc. We promote universal access to high-quality long-term care by encouraging private financing and discouraging welfare dependency for most Americans. We pursue this objective by warning the public about the risks of Medicaid Planning (artificial self-impoverishment) and by pointing out the benefits of good LTC insurance and home equity conversion alternatives.

Q. How did America's long-term care service delivery and financing system become so dysfunctional?

A. Medicaid was originally an afterthought, a tag-on to Medicare in 1965. Advocates for the elderly had huge political clout so they got a big, new social insurance program (Medicare). Advocates for the poor were much weaker politically, but they argued successfully that the needy should not be left out entirely. They prevailed, but achieved only a smaller, welfare-based program (Medicaid). The focus of both programs was acute care. But Medicaid contained a kicker, a provision authorizing payment for nursing home care for the elderly. No one thought this portion of the program would cost very much, because formal fee-for-service long-term care was still relatively rare.

The rest is history. The nursing home industry exploded in size to take advantage of this new source of money. Lax eligibility rules allowed families to place their frail elders in nursing homes on Medicaid at little or no expense. Home care, assisted living and private LTC insurance languished for decades for lack of demand and financial oxygen. Why pay out-of-pocket or buy insurance when nursing home care was virtually free? Medicaid long-term care costs skyrocketed even as the program acquired a reputation for inferior access and quality. Consequently, America finds herself at the start of the twenty-first century with a fragmented long-term care system suffering from institutional bias, an underdeveloped home and community-based services infrastructure, inadequate public financing, and low market penetration by private LTC insurance.

As Medicaid nursing home expenditures shot up in the 1970s and 1980s, our government began to clamp down on eligibility. Restrictions on asset transfers began in 1981 with the Boren-Long Amendment. Authorization for liens and estate recoveries came in 1982 with the Tax Equity and Fiscal Responsibility Act. Congress tackled trust abuses with the Omnibus Budget Reconciliation Act of 1985. The Medicare Catastrophic Coverage Act of 1988 made transfer of assets restrictions mandatory and longer. The Omnibus Budget Reconciliation Act of 1993 closed many loopholes and made estate recoveries mandatory. As soon as the government started restricting eligibility, however, the private Elder Law Bar began to offer "Medicaid Planning" to help prosperous seniors get around the new rules and qualify for public financing of their long-term care without having to spend down their assets. Beginning in the early 1980s, the rapidly expanding Medicaid Planning bar succeeded in opening many new eligibility loopholes to replace each one the government closed.

Finally, Congress and President Clinton became exasperated. They criminalized Medicaid asset transfers in the Health Insurance Portability and Accountability Act of 1996. This law came to be known as the "Throw Granny in Jail Law." It attracted a lot of opposition. Consequently, in the Balanced Budget Act of 1997, Congress let Grandpa and Grandma off the hook and targeted the real culprits with the criminal penalty. Anyone who, for a fee, recommended a transfer of assets to qualify for Medicaid became vulnerable to a $10,000 fine and/or one year in jail. But President Clinton's Attorney General, Janet Reno, concluded that it would be unconstitutional to enforce such a penalty. How could lawyers and other financial professionals be held legally culpable for recommending a practice that became legal again when the "Throw Granny in Jail Law" was repealed? Ecstatic Medicaid Planners quickly returned to marketing their artificial impoverishment schemes and the government went back to searching half-heartedly for new means to control these abuses.

Q. Isn't Medicaid an entitlement program like Medicare? Why shouldn't people manipulate their income and assets to qualify?

A. Medicaid is a means-tested public assistance program. It is welfare. Medicaid was intended to be a safety net for our nation's neediest. One is not entitled to Medicaid as one is entitled to Medicare, which is social insurance, not welfare. People qualify for Medicaid if they meet certain income and asset limitations. The intent of Congress and the expectation of taxpayers is that people should spend down their wealth paying for their own care before they look to Medicaid for assistance.

Medicaid Planners short-circuit the spend down process. They encourage seniors (or more often, their heirs) to impoverish themselves artificially in order to take advantage of Medicaid benefits without following the intent of the rules. As a direct consequence, genuinely needy people have a harder time gaining access to beds in quality nursing homes; heirs get early inheritances at the expense of the taxpayers; nursing home owners receive less than the cost of providing the care from Medicaid (according to the accounting firm BDO Seidman), and America's beloved World War II generation has largely died in nursing homes on welfare instead of aging in place at home.

Q. What is the likelihood that we'll ever see a government-financed model for long-term health care that provides for the middle class?

A. Nil. Social Security is in dire straits and will probably have to be at least partially privatized soon. Medicare has been bailed out by general tax revenues for many years, but it still faces bankruptcy in the foreseeable future. Managed care, long presumed to be the savior of Medicare and Medicaid, has undergone a severe backlash against inferior access and quality. Long-term home health care financed by Medicare was brutally curtailed in 1997. Medicaid's fiscal problems are legion and its reputation for access and quality is dismal and still declining.

In the meantime, private financing of long-term care has declined drastically even as public financing has skyrocketed. America spent $115.2 billion on nursing home care in 2004. The percentage of nursing home costs paid by the government (mostly Medicaid and Medicare) has gone up over the past 16 years (from 49.6% in 1988 to 58.2% in 2004, up 8.6% of the total) while out-of-pocket costs have declined (from 38.5% in 1988 to 27.7% in 2004, down 10.8% of the total). **(www.cms.hhs.gov/NationalHealthExpend Data)** The situation with home health care financing is very similar to nursing home financing. According to CMS, Americans spent $43.2 billion on home health care in 2004. Medicare and Medicaid paid 69.7% of this total and private insurance paid 12%. Only 11.3% of home health care costs were paid out of pocket. The remainder came from several small public and private financing sources. **(www.cms.hhs.gov/NationalHealthExpend Data)**

It does not take a demographic or economic genius to see what is happening here. The baby boomers are moving through American society like the proverbial pig through a python. When their generation approached adulthood, America got drugs, sex, and rock and roll. When the boomers arrive at senescence, America faces an equally dramatic cultural impact, but this time it will not be fun and it will be very expensive. With the major social insurance programs imploding already, having struggled only with income security and acute health care, what hope does the public have that government programs will survive to confront the much bigger future problem of long-term care? Answer: none!

The smart money is already preparing to take personal responsibility for LTC Planning. If enough of the smart people plan ahead, save or insure, it is still possible that some remnant of a publicly financed safety net for the long-term care of genuine indigents may survive. But don't count on it!

Q. *If the government isn't going to pay for long-term care, where can we turn? Many experts say LTC insurance is unafford-able, so our only hope is "social insurance."*

A. Experts like that still cling to an anachronistic social insurance model and ignore the massive empirical evidence that disproves it. Their argument boils down to this: widespread catastrophic nursing-home spend down and the unaffordability of private LTC insurance make publicly financed long-term care inevitable. Neither of these premises is true. Few people spend down their life savings before qualifying for Medicaid. Therefore, the public has little financial incentive to buy LTC insurance. That is what makes the premiums seem "unaffordable."

We used to think that 50 to 75 percent of all people in nursing homes on Medicaid spent down their savings to qualify. We now know the truth is that only 15 to 25 percent begin as private pay and convert to Medicaid. As low as these figures are, they include everyone who does artificial impoverishment to qualify for Medicaid as well as those who spend down the old-fashioned way, by paying for their own care. Actually, 78 percent of all peo-ple who enter nursing homes are already eligible for Medicaid and Medicaid pays for nearly 80 percent of all patient days in America's nursing homes. Historically, Medicaid eligibility rules have been so generous that the average senior, in terms of income and assets, qualified for nursing home care without fancy legal planning. Virtually anyone else, irrespective of wealth, could qualify easily and quickly given the right legal advice. These facts, not its cost, account for the low market penetration of private long-term care insurance.

Furthermore, private LTC insurance is not cheap. If every tenth house burned down, fire insurance would not be cheap either. This does not mean, however, that LTC insurance is unafford-able. Purchased when one is young and healthy, say between the ages of 45 and 65, good private coverage is available at afford-able rates. Even for a person over 70, premiums are nominal compared to the cost of a catastrophic long-term care need. You could argue reasonably that no one could afford not to insure privately if the financial risk were real. The problem is that easy availability of Medicaid financing after the insurable event occurs has anesthetized the American public to the risk of long-term care. Consequently, people do not think about private insurance until they are too old to obtain it or too sick to qualify medically.

Q. *All right, so how would you change public policy to meet the challenge of long-term care?*

A. The solution to the problem is clearly not more government financing. That would be like trying to put out a fire by dousing it with gasoline. Rather, the answer is to invite the public to look realistically at the risk of long-term care while they are still young, healthy and affluent enough to afford and qualify for private LTC insurance. To get them to take this danger seriously, we must advise people no later than when they apply for Medicare and Social Security that Medicaid will not pay for long-term care while they retain significant assets, that they will genuinely have to spend down to qualify, and that Medicaid only pays for nursing home care, not the preferred choices of home care or assisted living. Faced with a real risk, the public will buy private insurance to avoid the consequences of Medicaid spend down and to assure access to home care, assisted living, and higher quality private nursing homes.

Affordability of LTC insurance will no longer be an issue as people begin to purchase policies at earlier ages. Recognizing the need, seniors will consider reverse mortgages as a means to supplement their incomes in order to afford coverage. Faced with the loss of their inheritances, adult children of seniors will help their parents afford private insurance to protect the estate. Between the nearly $2 trillion in home equity held by seniors today and the $10 trillion their baby boomer children will inherit, there is more than enough wealth in America to solve the long-term care financing crisis with private insurance in a free market. If the government stopped destroying the market for private insurance by indemnifying upper middle class heirs for the cost of their parents' long-term care, we could unleash private insurance and save Medicaid for the genuinely needy.

Q. Why are many smart consumers avoiding planning for long-term care?

A. Most people fail to plan for long-term care because they think, "It will never happen to me." What they don't realize is that most people who need expensive long-term care are cognitively impaired. Half of all people over the age of 85 already have Alzheimer's Disease.

The fact that people are in denial about long-term care is not the most important point. Of course, no one wants to think about the possibility of becoming frail and incapacitated. Who wants to live in an institution? What interests me is the question, "How is it that people can be in denial about the long-term care risk when nine percent of all seniors will spend five years or more in a long-term care facility at $50,000 to $100,000 per year?" If Americans really faced a one in ten chance of being wiped out by a catastrophic long-term illness, they would not have the luxury to be in denial and they would plan ahead to insure against the risk.

That is the primary point I want to make. Medicaid financing of long-term care has enabled the American public's denial of the long-term care risk. Because Medicaid, with all its faults, has been there for the last four decades paying the bills after the insured event occurs, most Americans do not feel a sense of financial urgency about the risk of long-term care expenses. The solution is to encourage our fellow countrymen to take long-term care more seriously by assuring that Medicaid only goes to the genuinely needy.

Q. Aren't we seeing some positive changes?

A. Yes. For example, the president proposed a major reduction in entitlement spending, $10 billion of which was to come from Medicaid. Democratic and Republican Governors proposed achieving those savings by discouraging Medicaid Planning abuse and encouraging more long-term care insurance and home equity conversion. A battle of words and wills transpired in the Congress and finally, on February 1, 2006, the Deficit Reduction Act of 2005 was passed.

We don't have time or space to go into the details here, but we will be hearing much more about this legislation. It closes many Medicaid eligibility loopholes. It lengthens and strengthens the Medicaid transfer of assets penalty. It replaces Medicaid's unlimited home equity exemption with a maximum cap. It unleashes the Long-Term Care Partnership program for nationwide expansion. In a nutshell, this legislation sends exactly the message that is so desperately needed.

In conclusion: Long-term care is a personal responsibility. Medicaid is a long-term care social safety net but only for the truly needy. If you don't want to spend your own money for care, including your home equity, then buy long-term care insurance. Be part of the solution, not part of the problem.

If the states implement the DRA's provisions, and *if* the federal government enforces them, and *if* the media educates the public, we'll see huge beneficial changes in long-term care financing. But those are big "ifs," so we need to keep the pressure on politicians, public officials and news reporters at all levels to finish the job.

ACRONYMS

AAHSA	American Association of Homes and Services for the Aging
AARP	American Association of Retired Persons
ADLs	Activities of Daily Living
BBA	Balanced Budget Act of 1997
CCAC	Continuing Care Accreditation Commission
CCRC	Continuing Care Retirement Communities
CFP	Certified Financial Planner
CPA	Certified Public Accountant
DRA	Deficit Reduction Act
ERISA	Employee Retirement Income Security Act
FLTCIP	Federal Long-Term Care Insurance Program
HIPAA	Health Insurance Portability and Accountability Act
IADLs	Incidental Activities of Daily Living
LPN	Licensed Practical Nurse
LTC	Long-Term Care
NADSA	National Adult Day Services Association
NAIC	National Association of Insurance Commissioners
NCOA	National Council on Aging
NTQ	Non-Tax Qualified
OBRA	Omnibus Budget Reconciliation Act
RN	Registered Nurse
TQ	Tax-Qualified

GLOSSARY

— A —

Accelerated Benefits: A clause in a life insurance policy that allows payment of benefits for long-term care services.

Accumulation Period: The amount of time an insured is given to accumulate the number of days of care needed to satisfy the elimination period of a long-term care insurance policy.

Activities of Daily Living (ADLs): Physical functions that are performed on a daily basis such as bathing, dressing, eating, transferring, toileting, and continence. The ability or inability to perform these functions often determines whether an individual is capable of living independently. Long-term care insurance policies assess the ability and inability to perform ADLs as a criteria for determining eligibility for LTC insurance benefits.

Acute Care: Medical care received from licensed health professionals and/or hospitals with the aim of full restoration or rehabilitation of physical functions. Acute care usually refers to a treatment period of 100 days or less, which we define as short-term care.

Adult Day Center: A facility in which services and care are provided to individuals who are unable to remain at home alone during the day. These services might also include social and recreational events to alleviate the social isolation that a person living alone might experience. Caretakers who are regularly employed during the day frequently utilize these centers for those in need of care while working during the day. Senior centers and community centers often offer adult day programs.

Adverse Selection: The disproportionate number of people who are likely to submit claims in an "insurance pool," resulting in a higher rate of claims than expected. Results in the potential to have inadequate premium reserves to cover the costs of the claims unless premium rates are increased.

Alzheimer's Disease: A progressive, irreversible form of dementia that causes severe intellectual deterioration that eventually results in complete dependency. It affects 5% of those over 65 and nearly half of those over 80. The cause of the disease is unknown at this time. Symptoms begin with loss of memory and rational thinking, with progressive deterioration over the course of several years.

Ambulatory: The ability to move about, generally without any type of assistance.

Ambulatory with Assistance: The ability to move about with the aid of a cane, crutch, brace, wheelchair, or walker.

Ancillary Services: Personal care services such as podiatry, dentistry, and hair care that are needed by a nursing home or assisted living resident, but not typically included in the basic costs charged by the facility.

Assisted Living Facility/Community: A residential facility for those who may need help with activities of daily living, or supervision due to cognitive impairment. These facilities usually include private units (apartments or rooms), two to three meals a day, laundry services, transportation, activities, and housekeeping. In most facilities, a 24-hour staff is available to meet residents' needs.

—— B ——

Bed Reservation Benefit: A covered expense in most long-term care insurance policies that allows a facility to receive payment for a bed being held for a resident who requires temporary hospitalization.

Benefit Amount: A set dollar amount of benefit per day, week, or month that a long-term care insurance policy will pay for long-term care costs.

Benefit Period Maximum: The maximum amount a long-term care insurance policy will pay for covered services in a lifetime. The benefit can be expressed in length of time, or a dollar amount. This benefit may be payable to the owner of the policy or to a third party, such as a facility or home care provider.

Benefit Triggers: The criteria used by insurance carriers to determine eligibility for long-term care insurance benefits. The best policies "trigger" benefits when a policyholder is unable to perform two or more ADLs without assistance, **or** when cognitive impairment is determined to be severe enough for the person to need supervision.

Board and Care Homes: "Homes" that provide limited supervision and care to their residents. Medical personnel are usually not on staff and the administration of medications is not usually available.

Bundled Products: Policies that combine life insurance or some other financial product "bundled" with long-term care insurance.

— C —

Care Coordination: Assistance with the development and implementation of the plan of care including helping to identify appropriate services and making arrangements to receive care.

Caregiver: A person giving assistance to another. Assistance is usually required due to medical reasons, inability to perform activities of daily living, or cognitive impairment.

Caregiver Training Benefit: A benefit in a long-term care insurance policy that pays for someone to learn the best methods to use in caring for the policyholder who is on claim.

Chronic Illness: An illness characterized by permanency and/or residual disability requiring a long period of care.

Cognitive Impairment: Deficiency in short- or long-term memory; orientation as to person, place, and time; abstract reasoning; or judgment as it relates to safety awareness.

Co-insurance: The process of paying for a portion of the cost of care out-of-pocket.

Community-Based Services: Services designed to help older people stay independent and in their own homes for as long as possible.

Comprehensive Planning Approach: A 7 step process for planning for long-term care within the context of your personal and financial objectives.

Comprehensive Long-Term Care Insurance Policy: A long-term care insurance policy that covers care in any environment, including facility care and home care.

Conditionally Renewable: A policy that may be canceled at any time for various reasons, including excessive claims history. No longer allowed in currently issued long-term care insurance policies, but older in-force policies may contain this clause.

Conservator: If a court determines that a person is unable to manage his/her property due to mental illness or deficiency, physical illness or disability, drug abuse, chronic intoxication, advanced age, confinement, disappearance, detention by a foreign power; and if that property will be wasted or dissipated without being properly managed or if funds are needed to care for the individual or those supported by him, a "conservator" may be appointed by the court.

Continuing Care Retirement Community (CCRC): Also called "Life Care Communities," these communities offer the full spectrum of living and care arrangements, from independent living to nursing home care, without having to leave the community.

Custodial Care: Care to help an individual perform their activities of daily living, such as bathing, dressing, and eating.

— **D** —

Delayed Word Recall (DWR): A memory exercise that is used to screen for short-term memory or primary memory loss.

Dementia: Deterioration of intellectual faculties.

— **E** —

Elimination Period: Also known as the "deductible," the time period during which a policyholder pays for covered services before a long-term care insurance policy will begin to pay for those services.

Estate Recovery: When a Medicaid recipient dies and leaves an estate, Medicaid may seek to recover from the estate the money it spent on care for the recipient by using the Estate Recovery process.

Estate Planning: Addresses tax-efficient ways to acquire, preserve, and transfer a person's financial wealth to other parties, both during and after life.

— **F** —

Facility-Care-Only Policy: A long-term care insurance policy that only covers care in a facility such as a nursing home or assisted living community. Care in the home is not covered with these policies.

Facility Certification: A certificate given to a facility that is in compliance with a set of federal standards regarding staffing, cleanliness, and maintenance of records. Nursing homes must be certified before they are reimbursed for care provided to Medicaid recipients.

Financial Planning: The overall process of setting financial goals, evaluating where you are with respect to those goals, laying out a plan to achieve them, implementing the plan, and modifying the plans and actions as your current situation and goals change.

Formal Care Provider: Caregivers who are trained specialists and provide long-term care services as a career.

Free-Look Period: Also called the "Right to Return" provision. A newly insured long-term care insurance policyholder has the right to return the policy to the company within 30 days of receiving it, for a full refund of any deposits or premium payments paid.

— G —

Grace Period: A length of time after the premium due date during which the coverage remains in force although the premium payment has not been paid. This period is normally 31 days.

Group Long-Term Care Insurance: Coverage offered by employers or other groups that is normally issued on a Guaranteed Issue or Modified Guarantee Issue basis. This means that the applicant could be accepted for coverage without full underwriting.

Guaranteed Issue: A policy issued without any underwriting requirements. Coverage may be obtained regardless of current or past health conditions.

Guaranteed Purchase Option: A provision giving the insured the right to purchase additional coverage at set intervals without having to reapply and health-qualify for coverage. The premium for the additional coverage will be based on the policyholder's age at the time of benefit increase.

Guaranteed Renewable: A policy that can only be canceled because of non-payment of premium. Adjustments in premium may be made, but only for a whole class of insureds and not just the individual.

— H —

Health Insurance Portability and Accountability Act (HIPAA): Legislation effective in 1997 that resulted in the standardization of long-term care insurance policies and clarified the tax treatment of benefits and premiums for long-term care insurance.

Home Care: Personal care services provided by trained but non-skilled personnel. Does not require the supervision of a physician.

Home-Care-Only Policy: A policy that does not cover care in any type of facility. Typically, covers home health care, home care, and some homemaker services.

Home Health Agency: A private or public agency that specializes in providing skilled nurses, homemakers, home health aides and therapeutic services (e.g., physical therapy) in an individual's home.

Home Health Care: Care or services received from skilled personnel in your home. The treatment or plan of care is supervised by a physician or registered nurse.

Hospice Care: A special way of caring for the needs of a terminally ill patient and emotionally supporting his or her family. This care addresses physical, spiritual, emotional, psychological, social, financial, and legal needs, while enhancing the dying person's quality of life.

— I —

Incidental Activities of Daily Living (IADLs): Activities such as cooking, cleaning, shopping, laundry, managing money, administering medications, and providing transportation.

Inflation Protection Rider: An option on a long-term care insurance policy that provides for automatic increases in benefit levels to hedge against inflationary increases in long-term care service costs.

Informal Caregivers: Caregivers who care for a patient out of love or a sense of duty rather than as a profession.

Institutionalization: To admit a person into a facility, such as a nursing home, where they will usually have an extended or indefinite stay.

Intermediate Care: Provided when recovery and rehabilitation are the primary goals and 24-hour-a-day physician supervision is not needed.

— L —

Lapse: Termination of a policy when a premium is not paid.

Life Care Arrangement or Life Care Contract: Typically, a financial arrangement utilized by Continuing Care Retirement Communities. The resident pays an initial lump sum of money when they move in, and then a predetermined monthly amount thereafter.

Lifetime Policy: A long-term care insurance policy in which there is no maximum limit to the cumulative benefits that can be collected.

Lifetime Maximum Benefit: The term used to describe the total dollar amount that can be collected from a long-term care insurance policy. Choices in the lifetime maximum range from as short as one year to unlimited coverage, which has no cumulative dollar or time limit.

Limited Pay: Long-term care insurance policies in which premiums are paid for a limited time period instead of over the life of the policy. Common periods include single payment, five-year pay, ten-year pay, and twenty-year pay.

Long-Term Care: Medical and social care given to individuals with a chronic illness, disability, or cognitive disorder. Defined by the author as needing assistance for longer than 100 days. This care may take place in a skilled nursing facility, assisted living community, adult day center, the home of the person receiving care, or someone else's home. Care can be administered by medical professionals or nonprofessional personnel.

Long-Term Care Plan: The result of the process of deliberately choosing the most appropriate resources to pay for long-term care **in advance** of the need for care. The plan should be in writing and a copy provided to family members and financial advisors.

— **M** —

Meals-On-Wheels: A program that delivers meals to people who are homebound.

Medicaid: A welfare program administered by the federal and individual state governments that helps pay for certain types of medical care given to needy and low-income people. A nursing home must be certified by Medicaid in order to be reimbursed for care provided to a Medicaid recipient.

Medi-Cal: The Medicaid program in California.

Medicare: A federal health insurance program that pays for health care for people over 65 and some people under 65 who are disabled. Part A is Hospital Insurance and Part B is Medical Insurance. Medicare pays for limited short-term care in a skilled nursing facility but only under certain conditions. Medicare **DOES NOT** pay for long-term care.

Medicare Supplement Insurance: Private insurance policies that cover health care costs not fully covered by Medicare. Medicare supplement insurance **DOES NOT** pay for long-term care.

Medigap Insurance: Another name for Medicare supplement insurance.

Modified Guaranteed Issue: People who are in poor health but can certify that they are currently not needing long-term care services, or do not have a condition that will result in the need for long-term care in the near future, may qualify for coverage under this type of issue.

— N —

National Association of Insurance Commissioners (NAIC): A membership organization of state insurance commissioners. One of its goals is to promote uniformity of state regulation and legislation related to insurance.

Nonforfeiture Benefit: Usually available as an option, it allows the policy-holder to receive some type of benefit if the policy lapses. The benefit is usually in the form of a paid-up maximum benefit equal to the cumulative premiums paid at the time of the lapse.

Non-Tax-Qualified Policies (NTQ): Policies that do not conform to HIPAA's requirements and do not receive the same favorable tax treatment as Tax-Qualified policies.

Nursing Home: A licensed facility that provides general nursing care to those who are chronically ill or unable to take care of daily living needs.

— O —

Outline of Coverage: A description of the coverage and benefits of a long-term care insurance policy. Includes a statement of exclusions; limitations in the policy; a statement of the terms under which the policy may be returned and the premiums refunded; and a description of the policy benefits.

— P —

Partnership Policy: A type of policy that allows you to protect some of your assets if you apply for Medicaid after using your policy's benefits. Currently available in some states.

Plan of Care: An organized schedule of treatment or care for a patient, usually developed by care coordinators, physicians, nurses, or discharge planners at hospitals.

Planning Gap: A shortfall between the resources allocated to meet long-term care costs and the estimated cost of that care.

Power of Attorney: A written agreement that authorizes a relative, attorney, business associate, friend, or another person to sign documents and enter into transactions on behalf of the individual.

— R —

Respite Care: The in-home care given to a chronically ill beneficiary in order to give the regular caregiver(s) a break.

Restoration of Benefits Rider: If you elect this rider when you buy a policy with less than an "Unlimited Benefit Maximum," and you use a portion of your policy benefits, the entire pool of benefits in the policy will be restored if your health returns and you go without care for a specified period of time.

— S —

Sandwich Generation: A family that is raising children and caring for an aging parent(s) at the same time.

Senility: Mental deterioration that sometimes accompanies aging.

Senior Center: A community-based facility that provides seniors with activities such as recreation, education, cultural, and social events.

Short-Term Care: Care that is required for less than 100 days.

Single Sales Approach: Addressing one aspect of insurance or financial planning in a vacuum instead of considering all aspects within the context of the overall personal and financial situation and objectives of the individual, family or company.

Skilled Care: Care provided by a trained medical person and under the supervision of a doctor or other qualified medical person.

Skilled Nursing Facility (SNF): A facility providing skilled care by licensed staff.

Sponsored Long-Term Care Insurance: Offered by an employer or other "group," but unlike true group insurance, sponsored programs use the same strict underwriting guidelines as individually issued policies.

Spousal Discount: If husband and wife or partners purchase coverage from the same insurance carrier, they may receive a premium discount on both policies.

Survivorship Benefit: Offered as a rider, this provision states that if one spouse dies after paying premiums for a certain period of time, the spouse still living is no longer required to pay premiums on their own policy. Requires both spouses to have coverage with the same insurer, and normally requires that both insureds go claim-free for a certain number of years.

— **T** —

Tax-Qualified Policies (TQ): Long-term care insurance policies created by HIPAA legislation in 1996. Resulted in the standardization of long-term care insurance policies and the clarification of the tax consequences of receiving benefits.

Third Party Notification of Lapse: Requires insurers to send a notice to an individual designated by the insured before a policy is canceled due to nonpayment of premium.

— **U** —

Underwriting: The process of examining, accepting, or rejecting insurance risks, and classifying those accepted to charge the appropriate premium for each.

Uninsurable: Individuals who are not eligible for insurance due to the presence of a health condition that requires them to already receive care, or who may have a higher probability of needing care in the future. Examples would be people who have already been diagnosed with Alzheimer's Disease or Parkinson's Disease.

— **W** —

Waiver of Premium: A provision in some LTC insurance policies that states the insured is not required to continue paying premiums while he or she is on claim.

REFERENCES

American Association of Retired Persons (AARP). 2003. "Beyond 50.03: A Report to the Nation on Independent Living and Disability." Available as a download from **www.aarp.org.**

American Health Care Association. 2004. News release: "New BDO Seidman Analysis of Nation's Medicaid Program," February 4. Available as a download from **www.ahca.org.**

Congressional Budget Office. 2000. "Options to Expand Federal Health, Retirement, and Education Activities," *CBO Memorandum,* June. Prepared by the Health and Human Resources Division. Available as a pdf download from **www.cbo.gov.**

Douglas, Jennifer. 2001. *Long-Term Care Insurance: Trends and Outlook,* LIMRA International.

Employee Benefits Research Institute (EBRI). 2004. "Will Americans Ever Become Savers?" *The 14th Retirement Confidence Survey,* April. Retrieved from **www.ebri.org.**

Harper, Sarah. 2004. "Aging Society," *The Oxford Magazine,* March.

Hayes, Robert D., Nancy G. Boyd, and Kenneth W. Hollman. 1999. "What Attorneys Should Know About Long-Term Care Insurance," *The Elder Law Journal,* Vol. 7, No. 1.

Health Care Financing Administration (see The Centers for Medicare and Medicaid Services). **www.cms.hhs.gov.**

Health Insurance Association of America (HIAA). 2001. "Who Buys Long-Term Care Insurance in the Workplace?" October. Available as a download from **www.hiaa.org.**

Hewitt Associates. 2004. Press release: "Hewitt Study Shows U.S. Employees Sluggish in Interacting with 401(k) Plans," May 24.

Journal of Financial Planning, February 2001. "Coming of Age: The Shifting Dynamics of Elder Care" by Jacqueline M. Quinn.

Long-Term Care Financing Strategy Group. 2004. "A Vast Majority of Americans Over Age 45 Unprotected Against the Risk of Needing Long-Term Care, According to Second Annual Study." From *The Index of Long-Term Care Uninsured,* Washington, D.C., May 17.

LTCi Sales Strategies. Vol. 3, No. 2. Reprinted with permission. Available through **www.LTCSales.com.**

Merlis, Mark. 2003. Medical Expenditures Panel Survey cited in "Private Long-Term Care Insurance: Who Should Buy It and What Should They Buy?" March. Available as a download from **www.kff.org.**

Metropolitan Life Insurance Company. 2004. Press release: "Caring for an Aging Loved One at a Distance Costs Much in Time, Money, and Hours on the Job," MetLife Mature Market Institute.

Metropolitan Life Insurance Study. 1999. "The MetLife Juggling Act Study: Balancing Caregiving with Work and the Costs Involved," November. Available as a download from **www.metlife.com** (search Mature Market Institute for pdf report).

Metropolitan Life Insurance Study. 2001. "The MetLife Study of Employed Caregivers: Does Long-Term Care Insurance Make a Difference?" Findings from a national study by the National Alliance for Caregiving and LifePlans, Inc., March. Available as a download from **www.metlife.com** (search Mature Market Institute for pdf report).

National Alliance for Caregiving and AARP. 2004. "Caregiving in the U.S." Funded by the MetLife Foundation. Available as a download from **www.caregiving.org.**

National Association of Insurance Commissioners, **www.naic.org.**

National Council on Aging. Definition of "senior center" by the National Institute of Senior Centers. Retrieved from **www.ncoa.org.**

National Council on the Aging. 1999. "Americans Look to Employers and Government for Help with Long-Term Care," March 23.

O'Neil, John. 2004. "Easing the Burdens of Care." *The New York Times,* May 11. Available for purchase from **www.nytimes.com.**

Parker-Pope, Tara. 2004. "Health Matters," *The Wall Street Journal,* June 28.

Prenda, Kimberly M. and Margie E. Lachman. 2001. "Planning for the Future: A Life Management Strategy," *Psychology and Aging,* Vol. 16, No. 2, pp. 206-216.

Rush University Medical Center. 2004. "Diabetics at Significantly Higher Risk for Alzheimer's Disease," May 17. Available as a download from **www.rush.edu.**

Slome, Jesse R. 2002. Paraphrased interview reprinted with permission from *Long-Term Care Insurance Sales Strategies,* Vol. 4, No. 4. **www.LTCSales.com**

U.S. Department of Health and Human Services. 2003a. "A Profile of Older Americans: 2003," *Administration on Aging.* Retrieved from **www.aoa.gov.**

U.S. Department of Health and Human Services. 2003b. "Family Caregivers: Our Heroes on the Frontlines of Long-Term Care," December 16. Retrieved from **www.hhs.gov.**

U.S. Department of Health and Human Services. 2005. *Medicare and You 2005.* Available as a download from **www.medicare.gov/publications/pubs/pdf/10050.pdf.**

U.S. Department of Labor. 2001. *Report of the Working Group on Long-Term Care,* November 14. Retrieved from **www.dol.gov.**

U.S. General Accounting Office. 2001. "Baby Boom Generation Increases Challenge of Financing Needed Services," Statement of William J. Scanlon, Director, Health Care Issues, GAO Report No. GAO-01-563T, March 27. Available as a download from **www.gao.gov.**

University of California. The Institute for Health and Aging. Retrieved from **www.nurseweb.ucsf.edu.**

University of Pittsburgh Medical Center. 2004. Press release: "University of Pittsburgh Finds That People Would Trade Longevity for Quality End-of-Life Care," May 19. Retrieved from **www.eurekalert.org.**

RESOURCES

RESOURCES ON THE INTERNET

Administration of Aging's Adult Day Center Resources:
www.aoa.dhhs.aoa/webres/adultday.htm

Alzheimer's Association: **www.alz.org**

American Association of Homes and Services for the Aging:
www.aahsa.org

Assisted Living Federation of America: **www.alfa.org**

Caregiving: **www.caregiving.org**

Center for Long-Term Care Reform, Inc.: **www.centerltc.com**

Federal Administration on Aging: **www.aoa.gov**

Health in Aging: **www.healthinaging.org**

National Association for Home Care
HOMECARE Online: **www.nahc.org**

Medicare: **www.medicare.gov**

National Alliance for Caregiving: **www.caregiver.org**

National Senior Citizen's Law Center: **www.nsclc.org**

National Family Caregivers Association: **www.nfcacares.org**

National Adult Day Services Association: **www.ncoa.org/nadsa**

Senior Alternatives: **www.senioralternatives.com**

Senior Care Resources, Nursing Home Report Cards Online:
www.seniorcarehelp.com

Superior LTC Planning Services, Inc.: **www.superiorltc.com**

Visiting Nurse Associations of America: **www.vnaa.org**

RESOURCES FOR CONSUMERS

Professionals Certified in the
Comprehensive Planning Approach
Superior LTC Planning Services, Inc.
7041 Koll Center Parkway, Suite 255
Pleasanton, CA 94566
Phone: 1-800-400-0577
Website: **www.superiorltc.com**

How to Protect Your Life Savings from Catastrophic Illness
Harley Gordon, Corporation for Long-Term Care Certification (CLTCC)
188 Needham Street, Suite 230
Newton, MA 02464
Phone: 1-877-771-2582
Website: **www.ltc-cltc.com**

The Complete ElderCare Planner
Joe Loverde (Three Rivers Press)

The Dilemmas of Dependency
Wendy Lustbader (Free Press)

RESOURCES FOR FINANCIAL PROFESSIONALS

Corporation for Long-Term Care Certification
233 Needham Street, Suite 230
Newton, MA 02464
Phone: 1-877-771-2582
Website: **www.ltc-cltc.com**

Long-Term Care Professional Designation
601 Pennsylvania Ave., NW, Suite 500, South Bldg.
Washington, D.C. 20004
Phone: 1-202-778-8471
Website: **www.ahip.org**

Superior LTC Planning Services, Inc.
Training and Certification in the
Comprehensive Planning Approach
7041 Koll Center Parkway, Suite 255
Pleasanton, CA 94566
Phone: 1-800-400-0577
Website: **www.superiorltc.com**

INDEX

A

Accelerated death benefit policies, 194

Activities of Daily Living (ADLs), 15, 16, 97, 151, 218

Adult day centers, 25-27, 36, 55, 111

Adverse selection, 82, 183-185, 188, 189

Alzheimer's Association, 33

Alzheimer's Disease, 5, 16, 19, 22, 33, 36, 39, 97, 116, 127, 130, 152, 203, 218, 260

American Association of Homes and Services for the Aging (AAHSA), 33

American Association of Retired Persons (AARP), 32

American Health Care Association, 34

Assisted living communities, 22, 23, 28-30, 32, 33, 36, 38, 40, 44, 59, 110, 111, 131, 204, 249

Assisted Living Federation of America (ALFA), 29

B

Bed reservation benefit, 204

Board and care homes, 27, 28, 36

Bundled policies, 194

C

Care coordination, 104, 105, 152, 155, 157-161, 176

Care coordinator, 155, 156, 158-160, 246

Care manager, 155, 159

Caregiver training benefit, 203

Cash method, 109, 110

C-Corporations, 171, 182

Chronic condition, 22

Cognitive impairment, 16, 26, 53, 148, 151, 152

Co-insuring, 103, 117

Financial planner, 1, 51, 63, 65, 68, 75, 107, 125, 197, 211, 221, 224, 238, 243

Financial planning, 65, 207, 208, 221, 224, 225, 238-240, 243, 245

Financial ratings, 75, 140

Free-look period, 149, 150

G

Grace period, 202

Group LTC insurance, 32, 182-185

Guaranteed insurability, 121, 128-130, 132, 133

Guaranteed issue basis, 183

Guaranteed renewable, 195, 198

Guaranty Funds, 197

H

Health Insurance Portability and Accountability Act (HIPAA), 168, 169

Home care, 19, 22-24, 26, 30, 34, 38, 39, 47, 52, 79, 108, 110, 111, 131, 152, 154, 178, 203, 246, 248, 253, 254, 257-259

Home care only policies, 110

Homemaking, 24, 152

Hospice care, 21

I

Incidental Activities of Daily Living (IADLs), 16, 152, 153

Income tax planning, 66

Indemnity method, 109, 110

Inflation protection rider, 118, 124, 134

Informal caregiving, 25

Investment planning, 66

R

S

Notes...